GEORGE WASHINGTON
AND THE MAKING OF A NATION

GEORGE WASHINGTON

BY THE EDITORS OF

AMERICAN HERITAGE
The Magazine of History

AUTHOR

MARCUS CUNLIFFE

CONSULTANT

RICHARD B. MORRIS
Gouverneur Morris Professor of History
Columbia University

PUBLISHED BY

AMERICAN HERITAGE
PUBLISHING CO., INC.

BOOK TRADE AND INSTITUTIONAL DISTRIBUTION BY

HARPER & ROW

AND THE MAKING OF A NATION

*Washington, his wife, and their foster children gather around a large map of the new
Federal City. Watching over the family is Washington's valet, Billy Lee (far right).*

FOREWORD

The British statesman William E. Gladstone once imagined a grouping of pedestals for statues of history's most famous men. One stood higher than all the rest, and Gladstone was asked to identify the figure to be given the place of honor. Without a moment's hesitation he named George Washington. The story well illustrates the almost unbounded admiration and respect America's Revolutionary War leader and first President has aroused among men of all lands. Yet Washington's selfless devotion to cause and country, and his blameless private life, has often made him seem remote and even unreal.

He was, however, a flesh-and-blood man—one who could enjoy a fox hunt or a merry dance at a ball, worry about a stepson's education, become furious at a subordinate general's incompetence, or take time out from wartime concerns to inquire about crops at Mount Vernon. In writing *George Washington and the Making of a Nation*, the distinguished British historian Marcus Cunliffe has penetrated the myths and presented a realistic portrait of the man.

Through the years, the reverence felt for Washington has frequently been expressed in art. The familiar (Gilbert Stuart's famous Athenaeum portrait and Emanuel Leutze's "Washington Crossing the Delaware"), the novel (a German beer mug that may be the first representation of the cherry tree legend), along with autographs, maps, and contemporary documents are here presented to form a complete visual record of Washington and his times.

On December 26, 1799, Henry "Light-Horse Harry" Lee, Washington's devoted friend and fellow soldier, rose at Philadelphia to speak of the great leader's death two weeks earlier. It was there that Lee, speaking for all Americans, for all time, said of Washington: "First in war, first in peace, first in the hearts of his countrymen."

THE EDITORS

RIGHT: *President Washington and an Indian chief pass the peace pipe on this commemorative medal presented at the signing of a 1792 peace treaty.*
PUBLIC ARCHIVES OF CANADA

COVER: *In John Trumbull's painting, Washington, spyglass in hand, stands on the battlefield at Trenton as an attendant holds his rearing mount.*
METROPOLITAN MUSEUM OF ART

FRONT ENDSHEET: *Ships fire welcoming salvos, as President-elect Washington is rowed across New York harbor to his inauguration in April, 1789.*
NATIONAL GALLERY OF ART, WASHINGTON, D.C.
GIFT OF EDGAR WILLIAM AND BERNICE CHRYSLER GARBISCH

TITLE PAGE: *Emanuel Leutze's monumental canvas depicts General Washington rallying retreating troops on the sweltering Monmouth battlefield.*
ART COLLECTIONS OF THE UNIVERSITY OF CALIFORNIA, BERKELEY

BACK ENDSHEET: *Washington offers his hand to the dying enemy commander in a detail from Trumbull's painting of the Hessian surrender at Trenton.*
Surrender of the Hessians at Trenton: YALE UNIVERSITY ART GALLERY

GEORGE WASHINGTON
PRESIDENT.
1792.

CONTENTS

	FOREWORD	7
1	A COLONIAL UPBRINGING	10
2	SOLDIER AND PLANTER OF OLD VIRGINIA	20
3	TOWARD THE BRINK	40
4	EBB TIDE OF WAR	60
5	FORGING A VICTORY	84
6	CITIZEN IN RETIREMENT	106
7	THE FIRST PRESIDENT	120
8	DEATH OF A HERO, BIRTH OF A LEGEND	138
	ACKNOWLEDGMENTS	148
	FURTHER READING	149
	INDEX	150

Virginia plantations were self-contained communities complete with a variety of outbuildings, river-front docks from which trading ships sailed directly to the mother country, and water mills.

UPBRINGING

In 1729 a Virginian named Augustine Washington made a visit to England. He was not a stranger to the country. His ancestors had been minor English gentry, with the right to a coat of arms—the sign of an established gentleman. His grandfather, John Washington, was the son of an Anglican clergyman who had made himself unpopular with the English Puritans. In the mid-1650's John had emigrated to the New World, where the family he founded soon took a respected place in colonial life.

The Virginia Washingtons lived as planters, married girls who brought them more land, and played their part in the community as magistrates and as Burgesses (members of the lower house of the Virginia General Assembly). But they did not cut their ties with England. Augustine for a short time had attended school there.

On this return visit, he thus was at ease as a man of affairs who was both a Virginian and an Englishman. Since this royal colony, the "Old Dominion," was the greatest of the mainland colonies in population and wealth, Augustine had a proud heritage. But his affairs were a little complicated. He owned land and was eager to own more but, like most of his fellow planters, he was short of ready cash. He had an interest in a Virginia iron furnace—in fact he had sailed to England to discuss the new business with investors.

When Augustine got back to Virginia bad news awaited him. His wife,

11

whom he had left to look after their three children, was dead. Although people were used to sudden death in the eighteenth century, the blow was a heavy one. None of the first three generations of Virginia Washingtons had survived to the age of fifty, and their wives also tended to die young. Yet life had to go on; children had to be cared for and widows and widowers usually remarried.

When the period of mourning was over, Augustine Washington found another wife, Mary Ball. Small and perhaps already a little plump, Mary was an orphan in her early twenties—almost fourteen years younger than Augustine. She was descended from a London attorney's son who had emigrated to Virginia about the same time John Washington was making the voyage across the Atlantic. Not highly educated, she had grown up as a country girl, and had inherited a modest amount of property from her parents. Augustine's social level, however, was somewhat higher than hers.

Augustine took his young bride to live on one of his Potomac River plantations, which later came to be known as Wakefield, in Westmoreland County. There, in a small, brick, one-and-a-half story house, their first child, a son whom they christened George, was born at ten in the morning of February 11, 1732. (When the calendar was revised in 1752, eleven days were added to correct the previous inaccuracy. His birthdate, therefore, became February 22, 1732, "New Style."

Lawrence Washington was a faithful friend and sage adviser to his half brother George.

George seems to have thought of February 11 "Old Style" as his proper birthday. In his later life celebrations were sometimes held on one day, sometimes on the other).

Several more children were born to Augustine and Mary Washington in the next seven years: Elizabeth in 1733, Samuel in 1734, John Augustine in 1736, Charles in 1738, and Mildred in 1739.

Little is known of young George's early days. We can guess that his father was ambitious and restless. For some reason he moved from Wakefield when George was a child of three, to another family tract farther up the Potomac at Little Hunting Creek. On this spot George was later to create his Mount Vernon estate. But at the time his home, then called Epsewasson, was a compact house, probably with a few cabins and outbuildings surrounding it. Fields were still being cut out of the forest, and the broad river was the main highway for travel and commerce.

When George was six the Washingtons moved again, this time to a third property, Ferry Farm, near the little town of Fredericksburg on the Rappahannock River. Perhaps Hunting Creek was too isolated; perhaps Augustine wanted more social life for his family, or better schooling for his youngsters. Whatever his reason for the move, it did not affect the two sons of his first marriage. (The third child, a daughter named Jane, had died in 1735 at the age of seventeen.) Lawrence and Augustine, Jr. were sent across the Atlantic to the Appleby School in Westmoreland, the same English school their father had attended. He seemed to be prospering. Although still not enough of a landowner to rank with the Byrds, Carters, Randolphs, and other great Virginia families, Augustine Washington had title to about ten thousand acres in Virginia, and was the master of some fifty slaves.

Then, again with a horrible suddenness, came illness and death. George was only eleven years old when his father died in 1743. His half brothers, Lawrence and Augustine, were able to help his mother sort out the intricate details of his father's estate, and decide what must be done with George and the younger children. By the father's will, two of the three main properties passed to the half brothers; Law-

rence, fourteen years George's senior, went to live at Little Hunting Creek, while Augustine, thirteen years older than George, settled at Wakefield.

For a time George, no doubt puzzled and forlorn, divided his time between Little Hunting Creek and Wakefield and Ferry Farm, where Mary Washington was to remain—a widow—until the day of her own death nearly half a century later.

What was to be done for George? Although his share of his father's estate consisted of Ferry Farm, some other property, and ten slaves, it was not a huge fortune. Unlike his half brothers, he was denied the advantages of foreign travel and an English education. He remained in the colonial backwater and the extent of his schooling remains a mystery. According to one story, his father arranged to have him taught to read and write by an educated convict who had been transported to Virginia. Another tale, perhaps more plausible, is that he went to a school run by a clergyman in Fredericksburg. From a few early notebooks it is clear that he had a knowledge of elementary mathematics and trigonometry, which would later be of value in surveying; some notion of geography, which at that time was a vague science (he listed "Colofornia" as one of the "Chief Islands" of North America); and maybe a little Latin. He read Caesar's *Commentaries*, probably in translation, and a fair amount of English literature.

At thirteen he was copying a collection of maxims meant to turn boys into polite adults:

Sleep not when others Speak, Sit not when others stand, Speak not when you should hold your Peace, Walk not on when others Stop . . . In the Presence of Others sing not to yourself with a humming Noise, nor Drum with your fingers or feet . . . When you meet with one of Greater Quality than yourself, Stop, and retire especially if it be at a Door or any Straight place to give way for him to Pass . . . Play not the Peacock . . . Let your Recreations be Manfull not Sinfull.

George's formal education never got beyond this stage. Unlike Thomas Jefferson and other fortunate Virginians, he did not go to the College of William and Mary in the colony's capital at Williamsburg. Neither did he learn French, which he was later to regret, nor become bookish like Jefferson or John Adams of Massachusetts. His education was about average for Virginians of his time. If his spelling was casual, so was that of almost everyone else. Education was something an intelligent person picked up as he went along and as he needed it.

Young Washington learned to shoot and to ride extremely well: he was later to be praised as one of the finest horsemen in America. According to Mason Weems and other early biographers (many of whom exercised

A mid-nineteenth century Currier and Ives print identified this Potomac cottage as Washington's birthplace. The actual house may have had a sloping roof and double chimneys.

lively imaginations in writing about the first President), George did all kinds of things, from organizing juvenile military companies to throwing stones and silver coins for amazing distances. By fourteen he was strong, tall, and energetic. Someone, probably his half brother Lawrence, suggested sending him to sea as a midshipman in the Royal Navy, but his mother squashed the idea.

Mary Washington was once praised as a great and wise influence over him. In more recent years, however, historians have described her as an ignorant, selfish, pipe-smoking old nuisance. Whatever her character, there is no doubt that George remained a considerate son. He followed the copybook maxim: "Honor and Obey your Natural Parents. . ." Yet once he was able to start out on his own, he and she led fairly separate existences.

George's mother was probably right about the midshipman scheme. As a London relative warned her, "any considerable preferment in the Navy . . . is not to be expected, there are always too many grasping for it here, who have interest and he has none." George had no "interest," no pull. There were better chances for advancement in Virginia. Although society there was quite sharply graded, it was much less so than in England. Many of the rich Tidewater families were of higher social standing than the Washingtons. They monopolized the twelve seats on the Council, or upper house of the colonial General Assem-

The story of George Washington chopping down the cherry tree was told in Germany where a mug marked GW, 1776 was made.

bly, and considered themselves a cut above the Burgesses of the lower house. Still, there was plenty of opportunity to move up in society.

Virginia was, as George Washington said in 1760, "an infant, woody country"—as its name might imply, virgin territory. A man of ability, with good connections, could still carve out a domain for himself. He could acquire a handsome tobacco plantation on one of the deep rivers—Potomac, Rappahannock, York, and James, as they lay from north to south—where Virginia's life and wealth were concentrated. He could extend his hold by buying tracts elsewhere.

Little by little, as a man of ambition, Washington could take his place among the leaders. He could marry into a wealthy planter family. He could prove his worth in the community by acting as a justice of the peace, a sheriff, a military officer, or a vestryman in the established Anglican (later Episcopalian) church. He could impress the voters in his county (and treat them to drinks) in the hope of being made a Burgess. Eventually he might even win a seat on the Council.

The successful Virginian could live like a gentleman, importing his furniture, his best clothes, his books, and his wine from England, and yet feel that he was a pioneer. He could have fine horses, his own pack of hounds, scores and even hundreds of Negro slaves. He could buy the labor of convicts or indentured servants sent from the shores of the mother country.

On visits to Williamsburg or one of the colony's few other towns such as Hampton, Yorktown, or Norfolk, or to Annapolis in Maryland, a colonial gentleman could enjoy himself at dances and horse races, playing whist or taking his chance at lotteries. He could keep agents in the back country to seek out promising lands, and go there on trips himself. In eighteenth-century Virginia a man could live both stylishly and adventurously.

The chief help in George's formative years came from the friendship of his elder half brother, Lawrence. To him Lawrence was a glamorous hero, one who had served as an officer under Admiral Edward Vernon in the bold though ill-fated British attack of 1741 on the Spanish port of Cartagena in what is now known as Colombia.

When he inherited Epsewasson, the Hunting Creek plantation, Lawrence renamed it Mount Vernon as a token of esteem for his former commander.

By 1748 George came to spend more time at Mount Vernon. He was sixteen and the world was opening up for him. He could feel like a man among men, and a young gentleman among gentlemen.

Lawrence Washington was married to Anne Fairfax, the daughter of Colonel William Fairfax from the neighboring plantation of Belvoir. Anne was a lively young woman and George was drawn into a gay, sophisticated existence. He learned the social graces—dancing, card-playing, and billiards.

And George began to pay attention to girls, and to write half-joking, half-serious little letters and poems about them. In his correspondence with other young male friends he mentioned a mysterious "Low Land Beauty," perhaps a visiting belle from the Tidewater, and then a Miss Betsy Fauntleroy who took his fancy. There was also Sally Cary, a girl two years older than he. At eighteen she married the eldest son of Colonel Fairfax and came to live at Belvoir. George's letters show that he liked her enormously; he may even have been in love with her.

But the importance of the Fairfaxes to Washington was that they were powerful. Colonel Fairfax, a member of the Virginia Council, was the cousin of Lord Fairfax, an Eng-

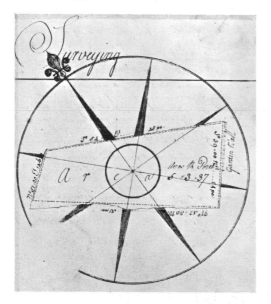

At thirteen, Washington listed in his copy-book a series of rules on conduct (above), frugally using both sides of the thin paper. His 1747 survey of Lawrence Washington's turnip field (below) is more legible.

lish nobleman who had inherited the proprietorship of Virginia's Northern Neck, a huge tract of land between the Potomac and Rappahannock rivers. The Proprietor fought a long legal battle over the boundaries of his land, which came out in his favor. In 1745 it was decided that Lord Fairfax owned about five million acres, including a large part of the Shenandoah Valley.

Uncertainty over land ownership had held up settlement of western Virginia. So, of course, had the presence of Indian tribes. Speculators had hesitated to buy land in the disputed areas. Now the way was clear. Fairfax had won his suit, and through various treaties the Indians were persuaded to give up their claims.

Lord Fairfax arrived from England to inspect the Northern Neck in 1747. He was the most important personage George had ever seen at close quarters; and Lawrence, already active in other land speculation, was a member of the Fairfax inner circle.

In 1748 George crossed the Blue Ridge with a party of the Fairfaxes to help in surveying their new wilderness kingdom. The journey was George's first glimpse of truly wild country. In one diary entry made during the thirty-three day trip he described "meeting thirty-odd Indians coming from war with only one scalp. We had some liquor with us, of which we gave them part." In another, he commented on the "most beautiful Groves of Sugar Trees and . . . [the] richness of ye land." The trip also gave him an op-

17

portunity to study the methods used by the experienced surveyor who was a member of their party.

Washington's interest in surveying began long before this trip. Using his father's surveying instruments, George had learned the trade from county surveyors. By August, 1747, he had acquired enough knowledge to handle simple surveying tasks, and his trip with the Fairfaxes gave him a chance to expand this knowledge.

He assisted in laying out the new town of Belhaven (later to be known as Alexandria) a few miles from Mount Vernon and just across the Potomac River from the city that would one day be named for him. He carried out surveys in different parts of northern Virginia. Along the way he bought title to two thousand acres in the Shenandoah Valley.

Then death again struck the Washingtons. Lawrence's family was sickly. Each of his first three children had survived for only a few months and the fourth child—a daughter—was not

well. Lawrence himself had developed a cough that turned into a lingering illness. At the end of 1751, seeking the cure of a milder climate, Lawrence sailed for Barbados in the West Indies with George as his companion. The change brought no lasting relief. Lawrence came home six months later to die of tuberculosis. George himself had fallen ill in Barbados of the dreaded smallpox, though he soon recovered.

In death Lawrence proved a lasting friend to George. By the terms of his will, his widow was to hold Mount Vernon in trust for their remaining child. If the child died, however, the estate would pass to George, if Lawrence's widow was willing.

And this is what happened. The child died, and George, while still in his early twenties, leased the property from the widow and was installed at Mount Vernon. He did not yet own it outright, but in time he would. Despite family sorrows, George's future was promising. Virginia was a realm wide enough to satisfy any man's ambition.

Nineteenth-century artist John Gadsby Chapman conjured up the image of young Washington in the romanticized painting at left. A survey map of Alexandria (right) was one of Washington's earliest commissions. The town's developers and their land parcel numbers are listed.

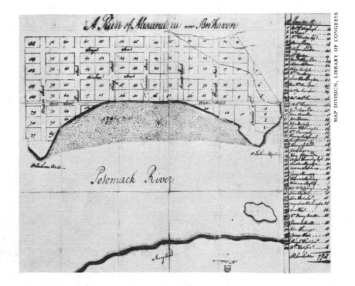

2

SOLDIER AND

To a Virginian like young Washington, there was one mortal enemy—France. Virginians were still subjects of the British Crown, and France and Great Britain were locked in a world-wide power contest throughout much of the eighteenth century. The rivalry had particular meaning in the colony, because the French barred the way west to Virginia settlers. No ambitious Virginian wanted to accept the idea that the land beyond the Allegheny Mountains was denied to him. Yet this was what the French claimed.

France's New World empire, on paper at any rate, stretched in a great curve along the St. Lawrence River in Canada, through the Great Lakes, and finally down the Mississippi River Valley through Louisiana to the Gulf of Mexico.

The French hold on this immense terrain was loose. Much of it was Indian country, and the only sign of French occupancy was an occasional canoe-load of fur traders moving from one lonely trading post to the next. But the French were careful to

Astride a prancing horse, an unflustered Colonel Washington receives orders from a mortally wounded General Braddock in this view of the 1755 Monongahela battle.

PLANTER OF OLD VIRGINIA

cultivate alliances with the more powerful Indian tribes of the region, and in the 1740's they were ready to resist what they regarded as encroachments by Virginians. The area of conflict was the rich Ohio River Valley, which the French claimed by virtue of the 1679–82 explorations of Robert Cavalier, the Sieur de La Salle.

On the Virginia side, the most active moves into the disputed territory came from a group of men that included the Fairfaxes and, before his untimely death, Lawrence Washington. In 1749 this group, banded together under the name of the Ohio

Company, received a grant of 200,000 acres from King George II. Still more land would be awarded if they managed to build a fort and settle a substantial number of families in the area within seven years.

The French were also planning to build forts in the Ohio country and decided, about the same time as did the Ohio Company, that an ideal location for one would be at the forks of the Ohio, where the Monongahela and Allegheny rivers meet. It was, in the words of a British soldier fresh from the relative comforts of England, "a desolate country uninhabited

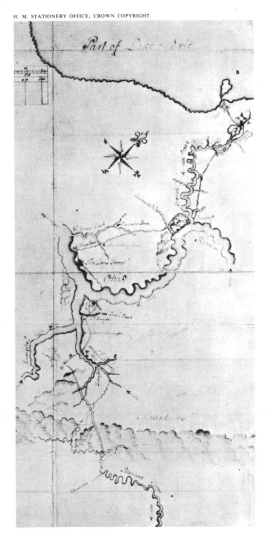

On Washington's 1753 mission to Fort Le Boeuf, his party followed the old Indian path through Pennsylvania shown in the modern photograph opposite. Washington's own map (above) indicates his route across the Alleghenies to the forks of the Ohio and then north along the river through French territory to a point just south of Lake Erie.

by anything but wild Indians, bears and rattlesnakes." Yet this wilderness was the scene of clashes that set off another major war between the French and British in their struggle for world power; and young Washington was soon at the center of things.

The future General's military career began modestly enough. In 1753 the governor of Virginia, a Scotsman named Robert Dinwiddie, received instructions from the home government to demand that the French withdraw from the forts they were known to be building southward from Lake Erie. If they refused, they were to be driven off "by force of arms." Washington, who had secured an appointment as an adjutant of Virginia militia a year earlier, heard of the intended ultimatum and volunteered to take the message to the French forts. His offer was accepted.

The mission was important, difficult, and dangerous. The young Virginia soldier had to find the senior French officer in the area, wherever he might be, and on the way determine by spying the strength of the French threat. He set forth in November, 1753; eleven weeks later he was back in Williamsburg to tell Dinwiddie what he had learned. Dirty and weary though he must have been, the news he brought was too urgent to wait. He sat up most of the night to write an account of his journey for immediate discussion by the Virginia Council.

In winter weather Washington and six companions (one of them an inter-

A 1754 map shows the British colonies hemmed in by French Louisiana and Canada.

preter, another a scout named Christopher Gist) had traveled nearly one thousand miles to the principal French fort, Le Boeuf, near Lake Erie, and back to Virginia. The French commander politely rejected Dinwiddie's letter. Anxious to convey this news and other information he had gleaned, Washington and Gist left their exhausted horses with the slow-moving party and covered the final stages of the return partly on foot.

A treacherous Indian guide took a shot at them once, but missed. Later, in crossing an icy river, George fell overboard from a clumsy raft, and spent a night in soaked clothing. Gist suffered from frostbite. But they reached Virginia safely. The report George wrote was so full and able that Dinwiddie is said to have praised him,

Lieutenant Governor Robert Dinwiddie

Christopher Gist helps Washington pull himself from the icy Allegheny to the raft on which they are trying to cross the river.

in Scottish brogue, as a "braw laddie." The Virginia Assembly was equally pleased. The report was even circulated in England and much talked about.

A few months later, in the spring of 1754, Washington again made news. This time he was a lieutenant colonel of Virginia troops raised to protect the construction of a British fort at the Ohio forks. Pushing west with a small force, he learned that the French were also on the move, and in considerable strength. In fact, they had already seized the forks and erected their own fort, which they called Duquesne in honor of the governor of Canada.

Friendly Indians told Washington that a small body of French soldiers was heading toward him through the forest. He took the initiative, leading his Virginians and the Indians in a surprise attack on May 28. They killed ten of the French and captured another twenty. Before Washington could intervene, his Indian allies scalped many of the wounded. Frontier warfare in America was especially brutal.

The little battle was Washington's first, and apparently to his taste. "I heard the bullets whistle," he wrote in a letter, "and believe me, there is something charming in the sound."

At the beginning of July, 1754, the situation was reversed. Colonel Washington, with a motley band of Virginians, South Carolinians, and Indians, was trapped by a superior French and Indian force. He tried to hold them off from inside the walls of a hurriedly built stockade which was christened Fort Necessity. His Indian allies vanished. The enemy maintained a steady fire until they had killed about thirty of his men and all his horses and cattle. At last he was forced to surrender.

Since the French were not officially at war with the British, they allowed Washington to march out unharmed, and he returned to Virginia. He was lucky that the French commander was so gallant, and able to keep the Indians in check. Otherwise, George Washington's scalp might have adorned an Indian hunting lodge.

Within a few months, when the Virginia Regiment was split into several independent companies, Washington resigned his commission in disgust and spent the winter months of 1754–55 at Mount Vernon. But before long he again heard the bullets whistle.

The French could only be dislodged from the forks of the Ohio by a bigger effort than the Virginians or neighboring colonists could mount. Two regiments of British regulars and some artillery were therefore despatched to Virginia, under Major General Edward Braddock, to oust the French from their posts on the Ohio. In June, 1755, Braddock's army began to move forward from Fort Cumberland (now Cumberland,

General Edward Braddock

Maryland), with Fort Duquesne as the objective. Washington accompanied Braddock as a volunteer aide.

The expedition ended in disaster. Progress was wearisomely slow; a road had to be hacked out through the forest for the wagons and the artillery train. Washington, ill with dysentery, had to travel with the rear party, while Braddock, fuming at the endless delays, urged his advance guard forward. His force, which included ten companies of colonial troops as well as the British regulars, was known to exceed the Duquesne garrison. An easy victory seemed to wait at the forks of the Ohio.

Then, when the leading files had reached the Monongahela and were within several miles of the fort, they were assailed by a French and Indian party.

Braddock was not exactly ambushed; he was expecting an imminent clash, but neither he nor his British

Washington signed a surrender drafted in French at Fort Necessity; the French commander and a British captain also signed.

27

redcoats were prepared for wilderness fighting. Jammed together in column, they were picked off in scores by unseen marksmen. The men began to panic. Braddock, riding back and forth on his horse to try and rally his men, was fatally wounded. Three quarters of his officers were hit.

Washington, though still weak from illness, hurried forward to the noise of the battle. Two horses were shot from under him and his clothes were nicked by bullets when he attempted to stem a retreat. But most of the British regulars, behaving worse than the colonials, he said later, "broke and ran as Sheep pursued by dogs." The enemy Indians, whooping, rushed in to tomahawk the sprawled mass of Braddock's casualties.

Fort Duquesne might still have been taken, for the main body of

British regulars, led by a fife and drums and followed by supply wagons, file along a forest road (above) on the 1755 march to the Ohio. On July 9, 1755, the advance guard (large rectangle in the diagram opposite) was attacked short of Fort Duquesne. The main British force was lined up below the path marked "A Dry Hollow Way," a distance from the ambush.

28

Braddock's army was still intact. But his second-in-command, unnerved, ordered a retreat that looked more like a rout.

The British defeat at the Monongahela had grave consequences. The frontier lay open to Indian ravages. Many an outpost was raided and had to be abandoned. Even when war with France was formally declared in 1756 things were no better. The home government had a global conflict on its hands and the fate of a few thousand colonial soldiers and civilians did not count for much in the general scheme. For the time being, the American colonies were left to fend for themselves.

Washington, much praised for his recent courageous conduct, was put in charge of Virginia's frontier defenses. He had the fine-sounding title of

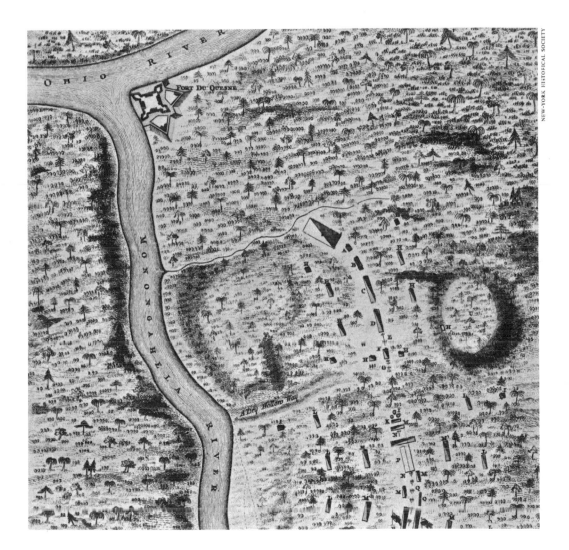

A cart conveys General Braddock from the disastrous Monongahela battlefield where he received the

wound in his lung from which he died. An army physician attends his wounds amid the army's retreat.

"Commander in Chief" of Virginia forces, but an almost hopeless task in recruiting, equipping, and training his men, and in placing them where they could do the most good. Not until 1758 was another expedition launched against Fort Duquesne.

Braddock's successor was another British regular officer, Brigadier General John Forbes. Washington was once more involved, and once more irritated by what he took to be the clumsiness of the plan of operations. This time, however, the goal was reached. In November, 1758, Forbes's men found the fort abandoned and in flames. The French had pulled out; they had given up the effort to hold the Ohio Valley.

Although the war between France and Britain ran on until 1763, the Virginia frontier was at peace. On the site of Duquesne rose Fort Pitt (after the British statesman William Pitt), which would one day give its name to the city of Pittsburgh.

The war was also over for Colonel Washington. For five years on-and-off he had served Virginia well and his military experience would stand him in good stead at a later stage in his development and that of America.

Strangely enough, these early military years were probably the most frustrating of his life. True, he had seen action and behaved bravely. But he felt that things had gone badly. He had resigned his commission once and had come to believe, perhaps unjustly, that Dinwiddie had ill-treated him.

Pittsburgh's first traces, beyond the walls of Fort Pitt, appear in this 1761 drawing.

Above all, his ambition to be granted a commission in the British Army was thwarted.

Throughout his service, Washington had been merely a "provincial," the holder of a commission from the governor of Virginia and not from the Crown. He had been paid less than a British officer; he had been outranked by and even looked down upon by regulars; the colonials he was expected to lead were harder to recruit and discipline than were the regulars. There was nothing odd in his ambition to hold a British commission. His admired brother Lawrence had held a British rank and in every way it carried more prestige.

Within a few weeks of his return

from the successful advance against Fort Duquesne, Colonel Washington's way of life markedly changed. In January, 1759, he was married. He probably wore his Virginia Regiment uniform of blue with red facings for the ceremony—and then laid it away in camphor. He was no longer a soldier, but a planter and a family man. He was twenty-six years old, nearing twenty-seven.

His bride was Martha Dandridge Custis, a widow with two children and a few months older than he. It is not known how she and George met, though it is on record that he visited the Custis home, White House, near Williamsburg, in March, 1758, and bought a ring a few weeks later. Whatever the exact circumstances, it was a good match.

The young Colonel was obviously a person of courage, persistence, and intelligence. He had the makings of a handsome estate at Mount Vernon—though in 1759 the property was much less elegant than the place that modern tourists see. He was, as he described himself to his London tailor, "Six feet high and proportionately made; if any thing rather slender than thick with pretty long Arms and thighs." George was, in fact, a fine figure of a man.

As for Martha, the information about her that stood uppermost in people's minds was that she was wealthy—perhaps the wealthiest widow in Virginia. The Custis family had long been prominent in the Virginia aristocracy and stood high in the favor of the Crown. Martha's inheritance from her first husband, Daniel Parke Custis, who died in 1757, was therefore substantial.

Her own property and that of her children, which George administered on the children's behalf, included several thousand acres of good plantation land, worked by several hundred slaves, and a town house in Williamsburg. These considerable assets allowed the Washingtons to live on a fairly lavish scale, and to extend the Mount Vernon estate by purchasing adjacent farms as they came on the market.

However, it would be wrong to suggest that George married Martha Custis for her money. All accounts agree that Martha was an attractive woman, cheerful and good-natured. She and George were obviously fond of one another, throughout what was to be a forty-year companionship.

They had no children, but George seems to have treated the two little Custis children as his own. The younger was a girl known as "Patsy" or "Patcy." Only three years old when her mother remarried, Patsy died at seventeen, to her mother's grief. The elder, "Jack," or "Jackie," was four years old in 1759; for both children their stepfather practically took the place of their real father.

Jack Custis was a charming boy, and perhaps well aware of his charm. George had him privately tutored for some years, then he sent Jack to a

A FAMILY FOR MOUNT VERNON

The portrait of Martha Dandridge Custis at twenty-six (left) was painted by John Wollaston shortly before she was widowed in 1757. He also portrayed her two children (bottom, opposite) that same year. Martha's wedding to Washington on January 6, 1759, is sentimentalized in the print below, in which she demurely joins hands with a statuesque George before a minister and guests. Washington soon brought his newly acquired family to his plantation at Mount Vernon (right).

35

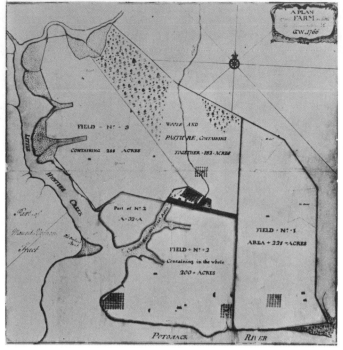

The survey map (left) of Mount Vernon's River Farm was made by Washington in 1766. The numbered tracts are cultivated land; the remaining plot is a pasture. Always interested in acquiring new holdings or investing for speculative reasons, Washington bought land in the Great Dismal Swamp (right, drawn by Benjamin Latrobe).

school in Caroline County, Virginia.

His stepfather frequently inquired as to Jack Custis's progress, and the replies became less and less gratifying. Jackie was "exceedingly indolent." What was more, he was "surprisingly voluptuous"—in other words, keenly interested in girls. The interest grew; though Washington entered his stepson at King's College (now Columbia University) in New York and took him there in person, Jack dropped out after one term, to marry (at the age of eighteen) Nelly Calvert of Maryland.

If George was now prosperous, there was no sign that he himself felt inclined to be indolent. To run Mount Vernon was a full-time occupation. True, its three main plantations were looked after by overseers, but they too required supervision. There were bricklayers and gardeners to hire, and slaves to look after.

Farming in colonial Virginia was not easy. Tobacco, the main crop at first, exhausted the soil and was in any case not very profitable to raise. Fertilizer had to be bought, and experiments made with new crops. After a few years George was planting wheat in place of tobacco. He needed to build a flour mill, and to find a market for the surplus flour.

There was a whole range of other crops and livestock for domestic needs. Provisions had to be ordered, and were consumed, by the gallon and by the hundredweight. The Mount Vernon community made its own shoes, wove its own cloth, and raised nearly

all its own food. His men fished for "alewives" (herring) in the Potomac. Salted in barrels, the herring were sold and formed a useful item on the credit side of his ledgers.

The diary that George Washington kept shows how much his concerns were those of a large-scale farmer:

June 7—[Rode] into the Neck, and went all [around] my Wheat there, which in general I think very good;
June 9—This day I went through all my Wheat at the Mill and find it very likely and promising.
June 27—Began in the afternoon to cut my Wheat at Doeg Run Quarter with Jonathan Palmer and 6 other Cradlers.
June 28—Elijah Houghton joined the above at the same place. The whole made but a bad day's work. They complain of the Straw cutting very hard.

When the weather was bad he stayed indoors balancing his accounts, corresponding with his agent in London, or studying agricultural treatises.

Gradually, he was able to leave more of the running of things to others, including his cousin Lund Washington, who became his manager. The laconic diaries show that George and Martha were drawn increasingly into the social life of Tidewater Virginia. They exchanged visits with neighbors, especially the Fairfaxes at nearby Belvoir. They attended church, went to weddings, christenings, and funerals, danced, played whist and another card-game called loo, and subscribed to lotteries. George had a pack of hounds and in the winter months hunted foxes.

37

It was a busy, varied, and pleasant existence. Nor were the Washingtons confined to Mount Vernon. He traveled to his and to the Custis plantations in other parts of the colony. Now and then he stayed with his mother at Ferry Farm. And he speculated in land.

One of Washington's major activities of these years concerned the so-called bounty lands in the Ohio Valley. These 200,000 acres had been offered by Governor Dinwiddie, back in 1754, to encourage men to enlist in the Virginia Regiment. Various complications delayed the distribution of the bounty. George, as colonel of the regiment, persisted in pressing the claims of his officers and men and in having the area surveyed. His own share was 15,000 acres, and he bought another 5,000 from veterans who could not take up the grant.

In addition, he joined a syndicate of influential Virginians who managed to secure rights to a huge tract in the Great Dismal Swamp area of southeastern Virginia. He visited the area a number of times, and he used some of his own slaves in drainage schemes to convert the Swamp into farmland. George also took part, with another syndicate of Virginians and Marylanders, in an ambitious (though finally unsuccessful) plan to petition the King for an option on no less than 2,500,000 acres of land in the upper Mississippi Valley.

By the age of forty, Colonel Washington of Mount Vernon was a Virginian of note. He was still not a member of the inner circle that made up the Council. But he was not far from qualifying for such recognition. Since 1758 he had been continuously re-elected as a Burgess, first for Frederick and then for Fairfax County. Then, as later, he was not renowned for his eloquence. It was men like Patrick Henry who enthralled the Virginia Assembly.

But George was respected by his fellows. Through his membership on important committees of the legislature, he acquired a good grasp of the workings of government. When he and Martha arrived at Williamsburg in their "Chariot" or family coach, to attend the "public times" when the legislature was in session, they were greeted by a wide circle of friends and acquaintances—the Nelsons, Lees, Masons, and others among Virginia's first families.

In his own parish, Truro, George served conscientiously as a vestryman —a task that entailed a wide variety of duties including looking after the parish poor. He was a justice of the peace, a Freemason (though not a very active one), and a trustee of the new township of Alexandria.

Although forty when he had his portrait painted, in 1772, by Charles Willson Peale, he was still slim enough to fit into his old Virginia Regiment uniform. Washington seemed a man of peace, a solid citizen for whom the whistle of bullets would remain simply a distant memory.

At right is the 1772 Peale portrait of Washington.

3

TOWARD THE BRINK

England's problems with her American colonies are parodied in this 1765 British cartoon. Liberty languishes at the feet of an Indian America; Britannia (seated) presents a box full of troubles; and the king of France (far right) offers a bribe to stir up new disturbances.

The text on the image reads:

Take this and let thy hand, Fall Influence be poured down upon them.

The S—p Act. 1765

What was known in Europe as the Seven Years' War, and in America as the French and Indian War, officially began in 1756 and ended in 1763. But in the Ohio Valley, George Washington had seen the war's early, disheartening phases.

The year he returned to Mount Vernon as a married man, 1759, the fighting, which had spread all over the globe, began to turn decisively in Britain's favor. It was a year of victories. By the time the peace was signed in Paris four years later, the French had lost all their colonies in America except for some islands in the West Indies. No longer could they stir up the Indians along the frontier. The colonists could take comfort and pride from the achievements of British arms.

But new sources of trouble arose from the British success. Some form of government had to be worked out for the former French provinces in Canada, now under the British flag. The war had been long and expensive. It had doubled the British national debt and there was much grumbling at the burden of taxation in the mother country. The young King George III and his ministers soon decided to organize the Empire on tighter and tougher lines.

As the London government saw the picture, perhaps rather harshly, the American colonists were not pulling their weight. Taxation in America was lighter than in England. The main war effort, King George III believed,

AMERICA'S LAST KING

During the rebellion of her American colonies, it was England's tragedy to have as king George III, who ascended the throne in 1760 at the age of twenty-two. The last monarch to rule America (opposite, in his coronation robes) was a conscientious, but dull-witted and emotionally unstable man. In 1765—the year of the Stamp Act crisis—George suffered the first attack of the insanity that was to obscure much of his later life. Sharing many of the king's own inadequacies was pudgy Lord North (caricature at left), who led the British government from 1770 to 1782. Intense believers in absolute royal powers, the two men were unyielding in a policy that regarded the American dissent as treason to the Crown and thus not subject to compromise. In contrast with the turmoil of George's public reign was his impeccably domestic and simple private life, one of fidelity to his stolid Queen Charlotte and affection for their fifteen children. Below, George *en famille* strolls the grounds at Windsor Castle.

OLD PRINT SHOP

had come from England. He and his advisers thought the colonists had been too ready to rely on British man-power and supplies. In the future, the Americans would have to pay their share of the cost of defending the Empire. This feeling was heightened by a sudden and serious Indian uprising along the western border in 1763.

In addition, the laws that defined colonial trade and taxation had been very casually interpreted. In theory the colonies were closely tied to the mother country and existed for her financial advantage. In practice colonists broke the law by trading with France and other nations. Smuggling was widespread. The Crown revenue officials were slack and sometimes corrupt. With horror the London government discovered, for example, that £6000 a year was being spent in salaries and other expenses to collect a mere £2000 in import revenues. A far firmer control seemed to be needed.

So began a new era in British administration. The first measure to arouse much colonial opposition was the Stamp Act of 1765, which imposed duties on legal documents and on various other articles. Patrick Henry in Virginia and spokesmen in other colonies protested. They argued that the act was unconstitutional because it taxed Americans without their consent. Only the Virginia Assembly, claimed Henry, had the right to tax Virginians.

George Washington made no public statement, but in correspondence

Defiant Bostonians burn documents and newspapers carrying the infamous Stamp.

he took the moderate, practical line that the tax would probably not work. It would annoy Americans; they would find ways around it; and even if they did not, there was such a shortage of currency in Virginia that not enough cash would be available to buy the stamps that the tax entailed.

Friends of the colonies in England saw the force of such arguments. Quite apart from the practical difficulties, they agreed that a principle was at stake. It was wrong to make the Americans pay *internal* taxes—taxes inside their own colonies—which they had not themselves voted. After all, it was on such issues that Parliament had fought against Charles I in the English Civil War only a century earlier.

George III and his cabinet were less sympathetic. After the repeal of the Stamp Act in March, 1766, they realized that money must somehow be raised in the colonies. The colonial legislatures, already ingenious at imposing their will on the royal governors, were showing more and more reluctance to tax themselves to meet the expenses of imperial officials. In 1767 Parliament, therefore, passed the Townshend Acts, which placed import duties on various basic items, including paper, glass, paint, and tea. The money thus raised would be used in part to pay the salaries of colonial governors and judges.

London insisted that the Townshend Acts were, unlike the Stamp Act, a form of *external* taxation, since the money would be collected at the ports of entry. Parliament believed that it had every right to levy external taxes, which lay outside the scope of colonial assemblies. Legally speaking, Parliament was probably correct, though clever lawyers in America disputed the claim. But the real colonial objection went deeper.

So long as assemblies had the right to vote (or refuse to vote) official salaries, they had some check on policy. The "power of the purse" was all important. But if a governor ceased to be dependent on his colony's assembly, he might overstep his authority.

These squabbles over taxation led more and more colonists to suspect that their rights as Englishmen were being taken away, or might be taken away if they were not careful. They were accustomed to running their own affairs. Why should far-off London now seek to dictate to them? Were they to be treated as trueborn Englishmen, or as inferiors, children, servants, or slaves?

There was still almost no thought of independence in the minds of men like Washington, or even of more radical spokesmen like Patrick Henry, or James Otis and Samuel Adams of Massachusetts. The measures they took—petitions to Parliament, plans

Further dissension in the colonies was caused by the Quartering Act of 1765—a law demanding free lodging for British troops.

to avoid the Townshend duties by agreeing not to import the articles covered by them—were a long way short of rebellion.

At this stage the colonists had many sympathizers in Britain. The home government seemed to be impressed by their case, and in 1770 all the Townshend duties were repealed, except for that on tea. Once more the excitement died down.

Yet the underlying cause of friction had not been removed. More was at stake than a squabble over minor taxes. Even if the colonists exaggerated their grievances, they were little by little, and quite unwittingly, moving toward the idea that they were Americans rather than Englishmen.

The process can be traced in the actions of George Washington. In 1765 he had been too busy with his own concerns to be seriously worried by the Stamp Act. By 1769, however, he and neighbors such as George Mason of Gunston Hall had begun to

Old Man Time projects a lantern image on a drawing room wall—a teapot exploding in the face of British regulars. This satirical comment on the Boston Tea Party is viewed by four symbolic figures: a grieving Europe sits between Africa and Asia; America is opposite them.

think differently. They were then ready to take the lead in a nonimportation plan that would cut off duties paid to England for goods sent to America.

Something must be done, Washington wrote to Mason in that year, to prove to "our lordly Masters in Great Britain" that the Americans were in earnest. If necessary, as a "last resource," the colonists could always take up arms to defend themselves. He introduced a set of resolves in the Virginia House of Burgesses, threatening a boycott of British goods and insisting that the right to tax rested with colonial assemblies.

Then came a lull. With the repeal of the Townshend Acts the need for a boycott disappeared. Washington occupied himself with plantation affairs. He resumed his orders from London merchants, including some elegant clothes for his stepson Jack Custis. When he took Jack north in 1773 to enroll him at King's College, Washington dined in New York with Thomas Gage, a British Regular officer who was a comrade from the days of Braddock's expedition. He was on friendly terms too with Virginia's new governor, Lord Dunmore.

In this peaceful interlude, Washington left political discussions to a restless minority of colonials. However, he had not forgotten his words to George Mason. If necessary, if colonial patience was pushed too far, defense against British oppression might be the only answer.

At the end of 1773 trouble again flared in Massachusetts. Stubbornly maintaining its legal theory, the royal government had left the Townshend tea duty intact without attempting to enforce collection. Britain now tried to exploit this situation. The East India Company, a powerful trading monopoly, was in financial trouble. London decreed that the company was to be allowed to sell tea (one of its main products) direct to the American colonies, instead of exporting it as before through private merchants.

Tea was then a popular drink—far more popular than coffee—in the colonies as in England. Thanks to the new monopoly, the East India Company would make a sure profit in America; and the colonists would get their tea more cheaply than before, even after paying duty, because the middlemen were being cut out. The scheme looked neat. Everyone would benefit except a handful of colonial importers, and the colonists would be lured into accepting the principle of paying duty as a type of taxation.

To the surprise and fury of the authorities, the plan misfired. In the port of Boston the merchants were enraged at being undercut by the East India monopoly. Radicals in the city saw through the British plan and denounced it. Acting in harmony with the normally moderate merchants—a novel and powerful alliance of interests—the political agitators staged the Boston Tea Party on December 16, 1773. Disguised as Indians, the Bos-

A VIEW OF PART OF THE TOWN OF BOSTON IN NEW ENGLAND AND BRITT[...]

tonians dumped 342 chests of the company's tea into the harbor.

If that had been all, Washington and his Virginia friends would not have sided with the Bostonians. He disapproved of the Tea Party as an act of wasteful violence. Virginians had different social and economic problems from those of Massachusetts, and had no great love for the Yankees. It was the British government's reaction to the Boston Tea Party that aroused Washington's patriotism. George III's ministers decided to punish the ringleaders of colonial resistance in Massachusetts.

In the spring of 1774 Parliament passed the so-called Intolerable Acts.

In this engraving by Paul Revere troops disembark from a British fleet anchored off Boston's Long Wharf and fall in along King Street. The stationing of additional redcoats in this rebellious New England community led to increasing tension after 1765.

By closing the port of Boston to all ships and dispatching large military forces there, London turned the town into an armed camp. The commander was Washington's old acquaintance, General Gage, but his friend, as the Virginian saw it, was now an enemy. Massachusetts could not be left to suffer such oppression alone.

The Virginia Assembly of May, 1774, protested so loudly that the governor dissolved it. But the Burgesses, Washington among them, stayed on in Williamsburg. Their behavior was polite, ironically so in the light of later events. They gave a ball for the governor's wife and Washington dined and breakfasted with Lord Dunmore as if nothing had happened. The two men chatted amiably about western lands.

Yet underneath, the situation was tense, and events moved rapidly towards a new climax. The Burgesses met in private at the Raleigh Tavern, formed themselves into an association, and agreed to meet again at Williamsburg in August.

By that time, Washington wrote to his friend George William Fairfax, who had recently moved to England:

it is hoped and expected that some vigorous . . . measures will be effectually adopted to obtain that justice which is denied to our Petitions and Remonstrances (and Prayers); . . . the Ministry may rely on it that Americans will never be tax'd without their own consent that the cause of Boston . . . is . . . the cause of

America (not that we approve their conduct in destroying the Tea) and that we shall not suffer ourselves to be sacrificed by piece meals. . . .

This was a private letter. In public George Washington did not say a great deal. Somebody described him in 1774 as "a modest man, but sensible and speaks little—in action cool, like a Bishop at his prayers." Still, he left men in no doubt as to where he stood. Back at Mount Vernon in July, 1774, he discussed the situation with George Mason. And he wrote strong letters about it. Some of them were sent to Bryan Fairfax, the brother of

A 1775 English print depicts a Virginia Loyalist being forced by club-wielding Patriots to sign a non-importation document. From a gibbet (rear) hang threats for the waverers—a tar barrel and a bag of feathers.

George William, who felt that the colonists were going too far. Washington replied that nothing was to be gained from the mild petitions that Bryan recommended:

Shall we . . . whine and cry for relief, when we have already tried it in vain? Or shall we supinely sit and see one province after another fall a prey to despotism? . . . I think the Parliament of Great Britain hath no more right to put their hands into my pocket, without my consent, than I have to put my hands in yours for money; and this being already urged to them in a firm, but decent manner, by all the colonies, what reason is there to expect any thing from their justice?

Colonel Washington returned to Williamsburg for the August conference. The angry Virginians decided to stop buying British goods, and—if their protests failed to have any effect within one year—to stop the export of tobacco or other products to Britain. Most significantly of all, they discussed the forthcoming general or Continental Congress which was to be held the following month in Philadelphia.

The idea of such a Congress had been first suggested in Virginia, and was warmly supported by other colonies. The Virginians chose seven delegates to attend. The Speaker of the Virginia Assembly, Peyton Randolph, was one; Patrick Henry was another; and a third was George Washington.

These were hurried, hectic days at the season of year when farmers were busiest. Riding back to Mount Vernon, Washington found time to write again to Bryan Fairfax, who like certain other Virginians was beginning to draw back from the prospect of serious trouble. George again went over the arguments that had determined his own actions:

"For my own part, I shall not undertake to say where the line between Great Britain and the colonies should be drawn; but I am clearly of opinion, that one ought to be drawn . . . I could wish, I own, that the dispute had been left to posterity . . . but the crisis is arrived when we must assert our rights, or submit to every imposition, that can be heaped upon us . . ."

When it came to taking sides, Bryan Fairfax, like Peyton Randolph's brother John and a sprinkling of other Virginia gentlemen, would choose to remain loyal to the Crown. Yet many Virginia leaders, for the moment at least, shared George Washington's belief that *something* must be done, even if a course of action was hard to determine. On the last day of August, 1774, in company with Patrick Henry and another delegate, he rode away from Mount Vernon, took the ferry across the Potomac, and set out for Philadelphia.

The Virginia representatives to the First Continental Congress greatly impressed the forty-eight delegates from the other colonies. Peyton Randolph was elected president of the Congress. Washington and his companions were obviously at ease at the public dinners that went on day after day: "more sensible fine fellows,"

Peyton Randolph (above) and Patrick Henry (below) led the House of Burgesses in attacking the Crown on colonial matters.

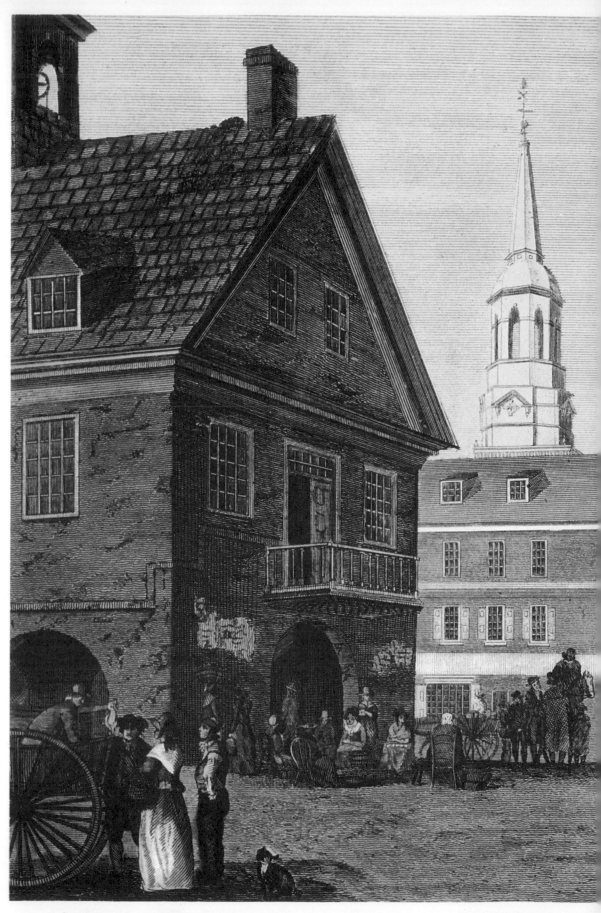

A familiar sight to delegates of the First Continental Congress was the bustle of activity at the

intersection of Second and Market streets in Philadelphia. Christ Church's spire is at left center.

wrote awkward little John Adams of Massachusetts, in slightly envious admiration, "you would never wish to see. . . ."

The atmosphere of the Congress was at first reserved. The colonists were not used to meeting with one another; it was almost as if they represented different countries. Some delegates talked far too much. Some seemed too wild and some too timid. Washington was one of those who struck just the right note.

Men from other colonies were awed by the Virginian's appearance, and by the rumors of his wealth. A story (untrue, as it happened) spread that at one of the Virginia conventions the Colonel had offered to raise a regiment of a thousand men at his own expense and "march . . . at their Head for the relief of Boston." What a princely gesture! Where there was so much boring oratory, his silence was all the more welcome. Not that he kept entirely quiet, of course: Washington made his opinions plain. He was particularly articulate across the dinner table and at small social gatherings.

As yet there was no serious talk of independence. George Washington wrote to a British soldier-friend of the old war days, now serving with the occupation troops in Boston: "I am well satisfied, that no such thing is desired by any thinking man in all North America."

The First Continental Congress was willing to petition the king once again, in the hope that he would get rid of his bullying advisors. The delegates asked for the repeal of the Intolerable Acts against Boston. They stated once more their view that taxation without proper representation in Parliament was unacceptable. They decided to import no more British goods after December, 1774; and if the Intolerable Acts were not repealed by September, 1775, they would try to stop sending colonial produce to Europe.

In other words, they had no entirely new suggestions to offer. The Congress realized how much division of opinion there was among the colonists. They presented a far from united front. What was new was the general animating spirit of the Congress itself, and of the sense of solidity its members felt from the mere act of meeting.

In all the anguish and confusion at Philadelphia, the quiet assurance of a rich soldier-planter like Washington must have been amazingly comforting. If such a man was with them, they could have reasoned, when he had so much at stake, their cause must surely be strong as well as just. Perhaps the Canadian provinces would join them, and Georgia which alone among the thirteen original British colonies had not sent delegates. In an optimistic mood, they adjourned at the end of October, 1774, having undertaken to meet again in May, 1775.

Virginia was seething with excitement when Washington came home to

Mount Vernon in the fall of 1774. In almost every county, including his own Fairfax, enthusiasts were organizing military companies. Several asked him to assume command, or help them with drill, equipment, and weapons.

Public opinion was so forcefully expressed that few were prepared to risk exporting their usual cargoes of tobacco or flour to England that year. The worried Governor Dunmore wrote home that Virginia was turning itself into an armed camp. The same mood was reported elsewhere. General Gage in Boston saw that his soldiers were becoming more and more unpopular with every week that passed.

In March, 1775, another Virginia

A European printmaker visualized representatives to the Continental Congress as a group of burghers transacting their business at a local inn. A casual atmosphere pervades the room as men smoke pipes and play cards. One man, wearing a turban, warms himself by the fire.

convention was held—this time in Richmond. The talk was of preparation to meet whatever crisis might arise. Washington along with two other veterans was appointed to a twelve-man committee that was to recommend a proper military organization for Virginia, county by county. And the seven delegates of the First Continental Congress were re-elected to represent the colony at the Second, scheduled for May.

Colonel Washington received more votes than any delegate except for the celebrated Peyton Randolph. He spoke and acted like a man with a mission, ready as he told his brother John "to devote my life and fortune in the cause we are engaged in, if need be."

That need was drawing nearer. In April, 1775, there was very nearly a battle between some of Governor Dunmore's men and militia led by Patrick Henry. Before the seven Virginia delegates set out for Philadelphia, stories had already reached the colony of fighting on April 19 outside Boston—the affair of the "embattled farmers" who clashed with Gage's troops at Lexington and Concord. The news was confirmed and amplified when Washington reached Philadelphia on May 9. It was said that a large army was on its way from England.

Although there were some doubters, the more than sixty delegates (representing all thirteen colonies on this occasion) were on the whole remarkably united. Even now they were not thinking of separation. The hope was to persuade the king, to whom they still pledged loyalty, to choose a fresh and friendly ministry. In the meantime, the colonies would defend themselves against British aggression. The Massachusetts soldiers who gathered outside Boston after Lexington and Concord were constituted as the nucleus of the Continental Army. Troops and supplies were promised from other colonies.

Colonel Washington was by now a key figure in Congressional affairs. Dressed now in the red and blue uniform of the Virginia Regiment, he was the man whose "great experience and abilities in military matters," as John Adams put it, seemed indispensable. Because a British landing in New York was expected, Washington was chosen to head a committee to work out plans to hold the city against invasion. In addition, he was put at the head of three other committees on military affairs.

When the question of a commander for the Continental Army arose, Washington was the obvious choice. He was, said a Connecticut delegate, "no harum-scarum ranting Swearing fellow, but Sober, steady and Calm." New England would be glad to have him, not only because he was a good soldier but also because the presence of a Virginia commander would give the force facing Gage a truly continental character. There was no other candidate who

Four leaders in the fight for independence were painted by two famous American artists of the time: Benjamin Franklin (below), John Adams (above), and Thomas Jefferson (bottom left) portrayed by Charles Willson Peale; and Samuel Adams (left) by John Singleton Copley.

St. John Honeywood's primitive water color based on an eighteenth-century engraving shows minutemen behind a stone wall firing on a column of retreating British redcoats at Lexington.

had such appropriate qualifications.

Perhaps Washington saw what was coming. He had not asked for the job, and when Congress nominated and then unanimously elected him a general and Commander in Chief of the Continental Army on June 15, 1775, he accepted with dignity but without elation.

He had not sought a quarrel with Britain, but neither had he dodged the issue. He was trying to do what was right. With typical high-mindedness he informed the Continental Congress that he would accept no pay as commander, but would take only his expenses. He would leave for Massachusetts almost immediately, without even returning to Mount Vernon. He contented himself with a couple of hurried letters to Martha, to assure her of his love, of his regret at being separated from her, of his having made a will, and of his firm belief that "it has been a kind of destiny, that has thrown me upon this service. . . ."

If destiny proved kind, the show of colonial resistance might still restore good relations with England. But there was no mistaking the fact that George III's ministers were for the present treating the colonial protest as an armed rebellion. By the rules of war rebels were criminals. If there were a battle outside Boston and General Washington fell into British hands, he would no doubt be sent back to England to stand trial, and might well be hanged. His old acquaintanceship with Gage would not

save him. But then, as he calmly reminded Martha, "life is always uncertain." The proud Virginian would never turn back.

On June 23, the newly created General rode out of Philadelphia to take up his command. John Adams was among the members of the Congress who went to the outskirts of the city to see him off. It was a stirring scene. Washington and his few companions were on horseback, and in uniform. A band played music and a troop of volunteer cavalry, also in bright uniforms, lined up to do him honor. All their hopes went with him.

It took Washington's party two and a half days to reach New York, where several companies of volunteers turned out to greet him. He remained in New York for another two days, gathering information, and then set out for Boston via New Haven. Riding at a good pace, but slowing to greet well-wishers, the party reached Cambridge, Massachusetts on July 2, 1775. Presumably because that day was a Sunday, the General waited until July 3 to assume formal command of the Continental Army that was penning Gage in Boston.

He may have been too involved in immediate problems to take note of the date. It was the twenty-first anniversary of the dismal little battle at Fort Necessity when he had been forced to surrender to the French. Whatever thoughts were in George Washington's mind then, surrender was not one of them.

4

EBB TIDE OF WAR

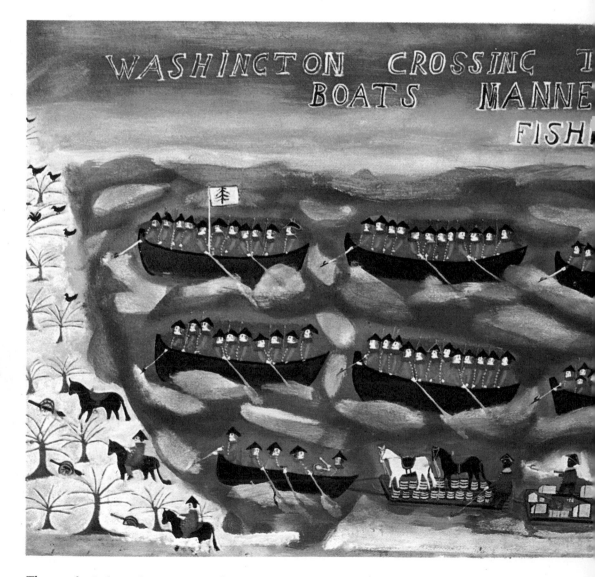

The war for independence was at a low point when Washington crossed the Delaware River to attack the Hessians at Trenton in December, 1776. In J.O.J. Frost's primitive painting of the famous

Two of the men who rode north from Philadelphia with Washington in June, 1775, Charles Lee of Virginia and Philip Schuyler of New York, were major generals. Congress had chosen four—the others were Artemas Ward of Massachusetts and Israel Putnam of Connecticut—to be senior officers in Washington's new army at Boston. Under them were eight brigadier generals: Nathanael Greene of Rhode Island, John Sullivan of New Hampshire, and six others of whom all but one were from New England.

The quality of these men who would help shape the destiny of the Continental Army was hard to gauge. Ward, in temporary command of the

DELAWARE BY MARBLEHEAD MEN

GEN. GLOVERS REG.

J.O.J. FROST
Nº 11 Pond St.

crossing, the General stands beside an American flag in the center row of boats. The rafts in the foreground carry supplies and Washington's omnipresent white horse toward the New Jersey shore.

General Washington, dramatically silhouetted by a puff of smoke, takes command of the American army at Cambridge.

forces at Boston, and Putnam had seen action in the French and Indian War. At the other extreme, Greene had had no more than six months' military experience, and that only as a private in the militia. Schuyler, a fellow delegate to the Continental Congress, was a rich patroon with a stiff unbending manner. Washington left him at New York to take charge of operations there.

Charles Lee, with whom he continued on to Massachusetts, Washington described as "the first officer in military knowledge and experience we have in the whole Army." Yet he was, as the new Commander shrewdly added, "rather fickle and violent I fear in his temper." Lee was a former officer in the British army whose political opinions had led him to join the Americans. He had fought in many campaigns and talked so convincingly that his new comrades were willing to overlook his grotesquely skinny, untidy appearance and his various peculiarities (he was so fond

of his dogs that he took them everywhere, even in to battle).

Another former British regular and convert to the American cause was Horatio Gates, who had been farming in the Shenandoah Valley of Virginia. Washington knew him slightly and persuaded Congress to appoint him Adjutant General.

The Commander in Chief's generals, then, were a motley collection. Still, several of them had seen as much service as he had, and perhaps they would not be too severely tested. When Washington wrote to Martha that he expected to be back home in the fall, he was not merely trying to comfort her. The Americans were optimistic, and on reasonably good grounds.

As Charles Lee had argued in a recent pamphlet, the British army was of uneven quality. Moreover, France and other European countries, eager to see Britain humbled and anxious to break her monopoly of American trade, would be likely to help the colonists. What was needed to show everyone how serious Americans were about asserting their rights, Washington and the Congress believed, was one quick resounding victory. If they could drive Gage's army away from Boston, their point would almost have been made.

By the time Washington reached Cambridge on July 2, 1775, it seemed as if this process had already begun.

At the Battle of Bunker Hill on June 17, 1775, the British army had launched a series of frontal assaults against stubbornly held American lines on Charlestown Neck north of Boston. But the one thousand trained soldiers the British lost in driving the Americans from their position could be ill-spared. Another such "victory" and the government in London might decide colonial resistance was too strong to crush.

A month earlier, on May 10, Ethan Allen and his brawling Green Mountain Boys from Vermont had surprised the British garrison at Fort Ticonderoga and seized the strategic Lake Champlain fortress astride the historic invasion route to Canada. If the Canadians could be induced to join the Americans, the British would surely come to terms with such a solid front of rebellious colonists. Peace could be restored; and George Washington could return to private life as a law-abiding Virginia planter, still a subject of the Crown.

Later in the summer, the Americans sent two columns north in a two-pronged invasion of Canada. Richard Montgomery's force from Ticonderoga occupied Montreal on November 13, and then moved down the St. Lawrence River to join an expedition from Cambridge under Benedict Arnold in front of Quebec. On December 31, the British repelled an assault on the city. Montgomery was killed; Arnold was wounded; and the American invasion was reduced to an ineffectual siege of Quebec that was lifted the following spring.

In the meantime, however, Washington was getting a rude shock after

This tense scene unfolds during a British charge at Bunker Hill: an unarmed Patriot, at the mercy of an enemy bayonet, is about to be saved by a comrade's quick action.

setting up his headquarters in the handsome Craigie House, five minutes' walk from Harvard College and just across the Charles River from Boston. "Continental Army" was an impressive name, but what it consisted of in the summer of 1775 was a scratch lot of 15,000 untrained and undisciplined Yankees.

The officers, elected by their men, had almost no notion of authority. Washington discovered a Connecticut captain giving a shave to a private soldier. He dismissed a number of officers for dishonesty and cowardice.

Although he felt that the men might fight well if properly led, he could not help noting that they were "an exceedingly dirty and nasty people." Their camps were squalid. They fidgeted at doing nothing, and many of them intended to go home at the end of the year when their enlistments expired. Although the Americans outnumbered the British, it was far from certain that they could withstand a really determined attack by a professional army that had the guns of a British fleet to support it.

In a few weeks Washington was

On a narrow spit of land below Quebec's rocky fortress, General Richard Montgomery is fatally wounded and his party turned back in the attempt to force the British barricades.

*A colonial artillery crew is
etched onto this powder horn
used in Revolutionary times.*
COLLECTION OF HAROLD L. PETERSON

reinforced by men closer to his own heart—thirteen companies of riflemen from Pennsylvania, Maryland, and Virginia. These "shirtmen" (so called because they wore fringed hunting shirts) were formidable figures. Daniel Morgan, for instance, had marched his company north six hundred miles from Virginia in three weeks. They were deadly marksmen with their long-barreled rifles. The New Englanders for the most part, like the British, carried unrifled muskets— short-barreled and less accurate.

One English soldier complained that the riflemen sniped at his sentries from behind trees and then slipped away. "What an unfair method of carrying on a war!" he protested. Unfortunately, Washington's new riflemen seemed to have even less idea of discipline than the Yankees.

The Commander in Chief did what he could to improve conditions. He labored to obtain more supplies of food, medicine, clothing, blankets, tents, guns, and ammunition. He introduced punishments almost as strict as those of the British. He insisted that the officers wear sashes of different colors to indicate their rank, and tried to teach the soldiers to respect their superiors. He fortified his lines, as far as possible, though he still lacked artillery. He even encouraged the New England fishermen to put to sea in small craft to harass the enemy. Washington enthusiastically backed the plans to invade Canada and held councils of war with his senior officers as to the best manner of attacking the British in Boston. Perhaps rightly, they persuaded him not to try.

By November, 1775, Washington was almost in despair. Although Gage had gone home, the British were firmly dug in; and Gage's successor, Sir William Howe, was thought to be a brave and skillful general. "Could I have foreseen," Washington wrote, "what I have, and am likely to experience, no consideration upon earth should have induced me to accept this command." His particular nightmare, then and throughout the war, was the struggle to hold together his troops.

The Continentals, in 1775, were extremely reluctant to re-enlist. The only way to get them to change their minds was to give them long spells of furlough, which dangerously weakened his force and tempted the men to stay home as deserters. Nor could they be blamed; their equipment was

65

Charlestown Neck (upper right) and Dorchester Heights (lower left) jut out toward waterbound Boston (center) as seen in this 1776 map. Washington's capture of Dorchester Heights made Boston untenable.

money or land or both, to attract them. The officers too must be well paid; this, he wrote in another letter, "will induce Gentlemen, and Men of Character to engage," and without such leadership little could be expected.

He was never to get his way, although the wisdom of his suggestions would be confirmed in time. There was too much suspicion of standing armies, which Americans thought of as dangerous to liberty. Later, Congress agreed that the Continental Army should be recruited on a three-year basis. Even that was not enough, and the pay remained low. The ordinary American preferred to join his state militia for six months at a time or a still shorter period, and with a generous bounty as further bait.

The result was that Washington and other field commanders of the Revolution never had a nucleus of more than a few thousand Continentals, even at the best of times. A miscellaneous group of militia, who were too amateurish to be relied on for continuous service, created an appalling nuisance because they were always coming and going.

Yet somehow the force around Boston was held together through the winter of 1775–76. Although the gallant efforts in Canada of Montgomery and Arnold ended in failure, the spring brought a renewal of hope to the American cause. In March, 1776, Washington—who hated inactivity and was always more ready than his

poor and their pay—when they got it —was only half that of the British.

As early as September 21, Washington was warning Congress that it risked having no army left. The "Military Chest," he added, "is totally exhausted. The Paymaster has not a single Dollar in Hand."

The whole concept of the Continental Army, Washington kept on urging, must be changed. Above all, it must be based on long-term enlistments. The ordinary soldiers must be offered a reasonable bounty, either of

Diversity of dress among colonial army soldiers was common. Two riflemen (left) wear fringed hunting shirts. The clothing below (left to right) includes a cavalryman outfitted for Washington's guard, the Commander in Chief's uniform, another rifleman, and a Pennsylvania regular infantryman. Above is a decorative Revolutionary drum.

councils of war to bring on a battle—went over to the offensive. It was a limited, but effective move.

Henry Knox, a stout, one-time Boston bookseller who emerged as an excellent soldier, arrived at Cambridge with cannon and mortars that he had managed to drag all the way from the captured Fort Ticonderoga. On the night of March 4–5, Washington seized Dorchester Heights overlooking Boston from the south, and dug emplacements for Knox's guns.

General Howe awoke from his long sluggish spell to realize that he had underestimated his opponents. With the newly positioned artillery, the Americans could make Boston un-tenable by bombarding it. Howe decided to leave, loaded his troops and about a thousand Loyalists on ships and on March 17, sailed off for Halifax, Nova Scotia to prepare for the year's campaign. He meant to descend on New York as soon as he was reinforced from England, and he meant to finish the Americans off before 1776 was over.

Boston was free again. The church bells rang and George Washington was a hero throughout the colonies. But his previous optimism was gone. It was obvious by now that the war was a real war. Reconciliation was impossible.

No longer did it make sense to

Sir William Howe (above) commanded British forces at New York. In a drawing of July 12, 1776 (below), the British fleet is anchored off Staten Island; the Narrows and Long Island are in the background.

distinguish between the king and his ministers. George III was as hostile as his cabinet to the Americans. Independence was the only answer. In January, 1776, Thomas Paine's *Common Sense* had been published and widely circulated through the colonies. "Everything that is right," Paine argued, ". . . pleads for separation. The blood of the slain, the weeping voice of nature cries, '*'Tis Time to Part.'*"

Not every American was of this opinion. Some were genuinely shocked by the proposal to cut the ties with England. Many others would side with whoever won the struggle. There was known to be a good deal of Loyalist sentiment in the middle colonies, especially in New York, where General Washington moved in April to meet Howe's expected armada.

In June, while Congress was taking the final decision on separation, and Thomas Jefferson's committee was drawing up the Declaration of Independence, British ships were converging on the port of New York—from Halifax, from England, and back from Charleston, South Carolina, which the British had bombarded in a rather half-hearted and unsuccessful expedition.

Since the enemy would have almost undisputed control of the sea, New York was nearly impossible to defend. In a strictly military sense, Washington realized, the best plan might be to burn the city down to the ground and then evacuate it. But that would cause great hardship to civilians; a gesture meant as defiance might be interpreted as defeatism; and in any case, Congress decided that the effort must be made to hold the city. Washington agreed, though he wrote to his brother that "We expect a very bloody Summer of it at New York."

The invasion force reached New York on July 2, the very day when Congress was voting to approve the Declaration of Independence. Ship after ship appeared over the horizon. Boatload after boatload of soldiers came ashore unmolested at Staten Island—more than 30,000 of them, the biggest army-and-navy operation of the century.

Several thousand of Howe's troops had been hired from German principalities, including Hesse. For this reason the German mercenaries were known in America as "Hessians." Britain used them because she was desperately short of men. But in the newly proclaimed United States the Hessians were thought of as blood-thirsty scoundrels, whose presence in America was one more proof of British oppression.

Altogether Howe's army, supported by a fleet commanded by his brother Admiral Lord Howe, was an awesome spectacle. Against it, Washington could only muster some 20,000 Continentals and militia. The British moved against the city in late August when General Howe landed 20,000 men on Long Island, meaning next to cross the East River to Manhattan.

On August 27, he engaged 8,000 Americans under Putnam, who stood in his path defending Brooklyn Heights. Howe made light work of driving off the Americans. Outflanking the first defenses, he took nearly 1,000 prisoners (including General John Sullivan) and inflicted another 200 or 300 casualties in killed and wounded—several times his own total loss. Putnam withdrew into the Brooklyn Heights breastworks.

The situation seemed desperate. Washington's immediate reaction was to fight, so he brought several regiments across the East River to Brooklyn to stiffen what remained of Putnam's position. Reconsidering, Washington rightly decided that he was in grave danger of being trapped. With a swiftness that was to save the Americans on more than one occasion, and helped this time by rain and fog, he ferried his whole army back across the river to Manhattan during the night of August 29–30. If Admiral Howe's warships had spotted the Americans' boats the war for independence might have ended then and there.

The respite was only temporary; Manhattan Island might prove to be another trap. Indeed, General Howe followed Washington across the river,

The subject of John Trumbull's painting is the moment at which the drafting committee (from left: Adams, Sherman, Livingston, Jefferson, and Franklin) presents the Declaration of Independence to Congress.

70

Dressed in their marching uniforms and unprepared for battle, the 42nd Highlanders scurry over a fence at Harlem Heights during Washington's surprise attack on September 16, 1776.

landing on September 15 at Kip's Bay (just south of the present United Nations). Unable to rally the fleeing Americans, Washington at one point was about to be surrounded by Hessian troops when an aide forced him to seek safety in retreat.

Yet, Howe failed to press his advance up the length of Manhattan, although no more than the width of modern Central Park separated the fleeing Americans from their British adversaries. On September 16, however, Washington turned on his pursuers at Harlem Heights and drove them off in a sharp little fight.

Washington explained his situation in a letter to Congress that month. The enemy, he wrote, meant to use their superiority in ships and men to "enclose us on the Island of New York." Bearing in mind that some of his raw troops might break under fire, he reluctantly concluded "that on our Side the War should be defensive. . . . That we should on all Occasions avoid a general Action."

New York would have to be abandoned, but by delaying tactics. It might be possible, however, to hold on to two places, Fort Washington on Manhattan and Fort Lee on the New Jersey shore, and thus control movement along the vital highway of the Hudson River.

For nearly a month after the Battle of Harlem Heights, Howe rested as the two armies faced one another across their northern Manhattan fortifications.

On October 12, the cautious British general moved the greater part of his force by boat further up the East River to make a new landing, first at Throgs Neck, then on the mainland at Pell's Point. Realizing that he was about to be flanked, Washington withdrew from Manhattan and marched toward White Plains, where he collided with Howe on October 28.

Washington again withdrew north to a new position and, when the British general failed to attack, crossed into New Jersey. Howe turned south on November 16 to capture the force the American Commander had unwisely left in Manhattan at Fort Washington and a few days later also took Fort Lee.

With his troops dwindling disas-trously, Washington retreated across New Jersey, and, on December 7, crossed the Delaware River into Pennsylvania.

The prospects facing Washington as 1776 drew to a close were gloomy indeed. Enlistment terms of his remaining troops were rapidly expiring, and if the British came after him in strength there was little he could do

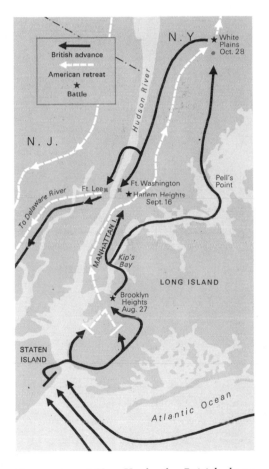

Converging at New York, the British drove the Patriots first from Long Island, then Manhattan. After White Plains, Washington crossed the Hudson at Peekskill (off map) and retreated through New Jersey.

74

IN THE ENEMY CAMP

England, like her colonies, was beset with a manpower shortage as the Revolutionary War began and, from the outset, hired German mercenaries (known generally, although incorrectly, as Hessians) to fight in America. Various Hessian regiments are represented along the top of the page. From left to right stand three soldiers of Landgrave's Third Guard, five from the Prinz Carl Regiment and two jägers (formerly hunters and foresters), and an officer and noncom of the Knyphausen Regiment. Discipline among all troops fighting on the British side was strict, although the camp at left is pervaded by an easy atmosphere; laundry dries on tent tops and ladies move freely through bivouac areas. (However, cannon balls and drums are stacked according to regulations.) Visitors undoubtedly were welcome, and in the contemporary cartoon at far left a bizarre trio is escorted through an encampment by a grenadier.

to stop them. His own reputation had slumped. Charles Lee, after ignoring repeated commands from Washington to hasten his own retreat through New Jersey, was finally captured at Basking Ridge by a British scouting party on December 13.

Congress, expecting the British to push on to Philadelphia, hastily departed for Baltimore. The lawmakers would make several such moves in the years ahead, and in the intervals when America had no effective government, General Washington was entrusted with almost dictatorial powers.

At this critical stage, Howe went into winter quarters in New York, leaving only token garrisons at various points in New Jersey. Washington, in one of his most spectacular strokes of the war, seized the opportunity to save his name, his army, and perhaps the entire American cause as well.

With 2,400 men, in the bitter cold of Christmas night, 1776, he rowed back over the ice-choked Delaware to the New Jersey side and launched a sudden attack on the Hessian garrison at Trenton on the morning of December 26. The enemy was caught completely off balance—indeed many of them were probably drunk from Christmas carousing. The Hessian commander and about thirty men were killed and more than 900 of his soldiers taken prisoner. Washington's casualties were only four wounded.

It was a sensationally bold stroke, and American spirits rose. At last they had something to cheer about. A British observer said they were "all liberty mad again." The British commander in New Jersey, General Lord Cornwallis, set out after the Americans with 8,000 men, found them on January 2, and triumphantly announced that he had "run down the old fox" and would "bag him in the morning."

But when morning came the "old fox" had disappeared, leaving his campfires lit to deceive the enemy. In-

General Charles Lee, captured by members of the British regiment which he had once led, turns over his sword to the patrol officer waiting outside a New Jersey tavern.

Though historically inaccurate in many of its details, Emanuel Leutze's painting of Washington crossing the Delaware is the most famous one of that renowned boat trip.

stead Washington pounced on a British force at Princeton, thoroughly alarmed Cornwallis, and withdrew calmly into his own winter quarters in the hills of New Jersey around Morristown on January 6, 1777.

It had been a brilliant little campaign. The British had once been inclined to jeer at the Americans as "raw, undisciplined, cowardly men." Such taunts were no longer being made—at least not by those who knew better.

The struggle for independence was beginning to reveal itself more clearly as an endurance contest. Washington's problem was to hold on longer than the enemy. With fewer resources he must make every man and every bullet count. He must somehow contrive to outguess and outmaneuver his opponents. In the face of all his daunting difficulties he must set an example of confidence and defiance.

By temperament, Washington was superbly fitted for the almost impossible task, though he longed to be able

Lost until 1953, this painting by George Washington Parke Custis portrays his foster father at the battle of Trenton. Washington, on his white horse, confers with General Greene.

to meet and beat the British in battle on equal terms. What helped to keep him and his Continentals going was the knowledge that no other road lay open. There was no further thought of bargaining with George III. Independence was the goal. Though at moments it seemed terribly far away, it had become a definite and magnificent war aim. Americans were fighting to be Americans.

After Washington's beautifully calculated attacks at Trenton and Princeton, General Howe remained inactive for several months. Congress returned to Philadelphia. Martha was able to join her husband at his winter headquarters in a Morristown tavern. (She would be able to spend a part of each of the next few winters in camp with him.)

The General kept busy with his endless burden of correspondence. To set a good example to his half-starved and ill-clad men, his tavern mess-table was frugally laid. No wine was served, though he was something of a connoisseur. More practical problems had to be attended to—for example, inoculating his troops (a treatment that was still something of a novelty) against the dreaded smallpox.

The British plan for the campaign of 1777 took so long to unfold, and was so peculiar when it did, that Washington was understandably puzzled. It was the product of divided views among the different commanders. Howe, centered in New Jersey, was determined to take Philadelphia,

in the belief that large numbers of Loyalists would join him.

General John Burgoyne wanted to strike down from Canada by the Lake Champlain-Hudson River route, retaking Fort Ticonderoga and smashing the force under Schuyler which guarded the way. An auxiliary force led by General Barry St. Leger, moving down the Mohawk River Valley from Oswego, was to join him at Albany. This would end the threat of an American invasion of Canada by the same route, and isolate New England from the other states.

A third general, Sir Henry Clinton, occupying New York, was too cautious to be happy with either scheme. But both were set in motion. To Clinton's objections that not enough troops were available, Howe could point to the speed of his 1776 advance on Manhattan; after taking Philadelphia, he would be able to send troops north to link up with Burgoyne.

Howe added to the mystification of the Americans, and to his own difficulties, by deciding to take his 15,000 troops back to New York and out to sea. When his transports finally set sail from New York in late July, Washington guessed incorrectly that their destination was Charleston.

A dilemma faced the American Commander. Burgoyne, who was known only to be on the way from Canada with about 8,000 men, had in fact already seized Ticonderoga and was confidently advancing south.

TRENTON: After crossing the Delaware some nine miles upriver from Trenton, Washington divides his army: Sullivan takes the River Road (1), as Greene moves inland along the Pennington Road (2). Driving in the Hessian pickets, Greene's men deploy (3); Knox places his guns so as to sweep King and Queen streets and the open ground east of town (4). American units swing to the left (5) to keep the Knyphausen regiment from escaping, while Colonel Rall's troops are cut down in the narrow streets (6). The Hessians, caught between Greene and Sullivan, are surrounded (7 and 8).

PRINCETON: Cornwallis occupies Trenton and prepares to attack Washington's camp along the Assunpink (1). After dark, the Continentals slip around the enemy flank (2), aiming for the British supplies at New Brunswick. En route to Princeton (3), Washington sends Mercer up the Quaker Road (4), where he is spotted by Mawhood's British marching to Trenton (5). Both sides make for a nearby hill (6) and the Americans are routed (7). Washington rallies them (8) and drives Mawhood off (9). Pushing on to Princeton, the Americans defeat British reinforcements at Nassau Hall (10).

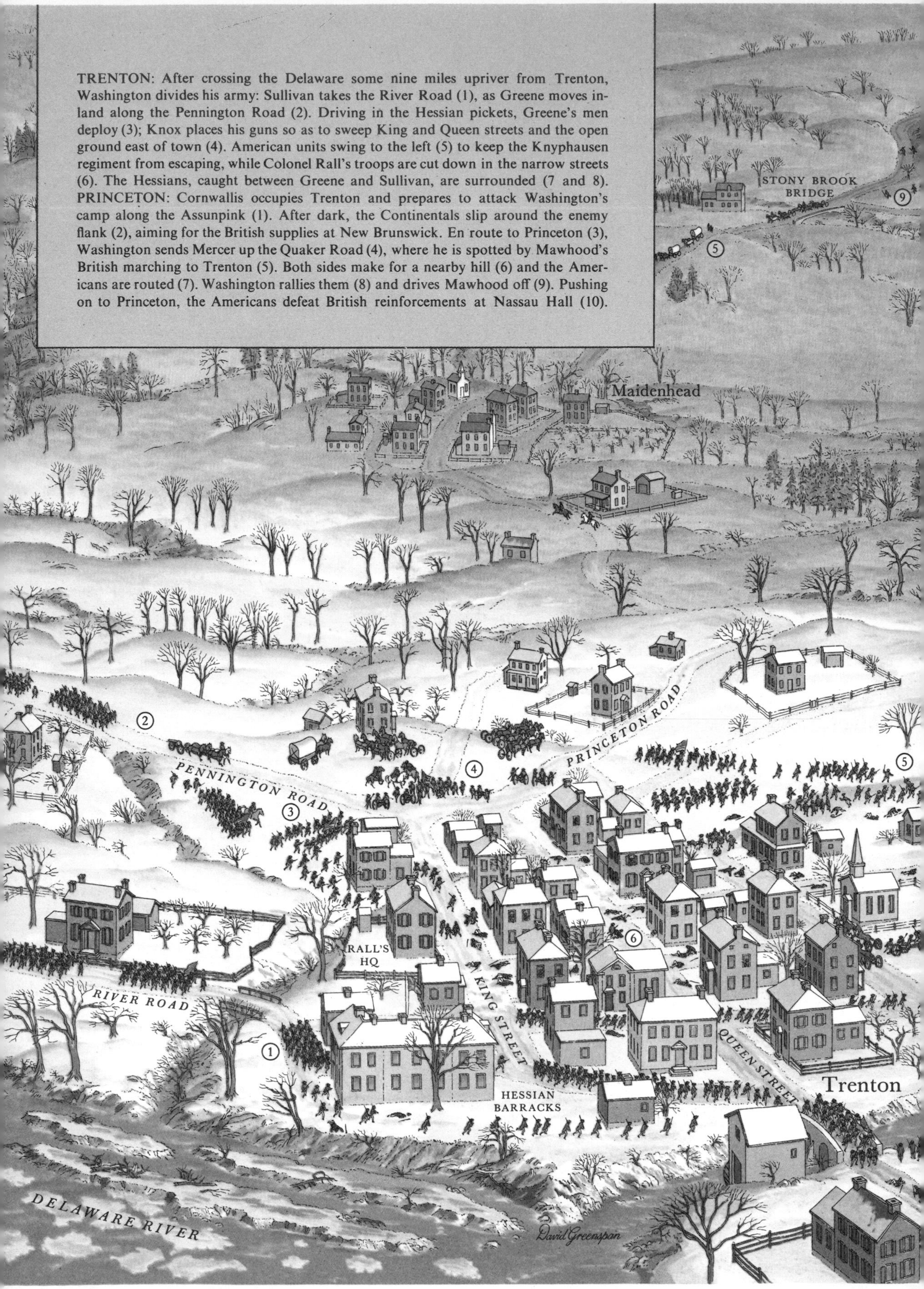

STONY BROOK BRIDGE

⑨

⑤

Maidenhead

②

PENNINGTON ROAD

③

④

PRINCETON ROAD

⑤

⑥

RALL'S HQ

KING STREET

①

RIVER ROAD

QUEEN STREET

Trenton

HESSIAN BARRACKS

DELAWARE RIVER

David Greenspan

TO NEW BRUNSWICK

PRINCETON ROAD

NASSAU HALL

Princeton

⑩

⑥

⑧

⑦

QUAKER ROAD

④

QUAKER MEETING
HOUSE

③

STONY BROOK

②

PRINCETON

January 3, 1777

QUAKER ROAD

TRENTON

December 26, 1776

⑦

⑧

SSUNPINK CREEK

①

DAVID GREENSPAN

Should Washington ignore Howe and instead march north against Burgoyne? United with Schuyler, he could be reasonably sure of beating Burgoyne.

Instead, with a generosity that some military historians have criticized, the Commander in Chief dispatched 500 of his own troops to join Schuyler and released a considerable body of troops from Peekskill for service in the north. Then he turned his attention to Howe whose destination now proved to be Philadelphia.

The main British army sailed in-

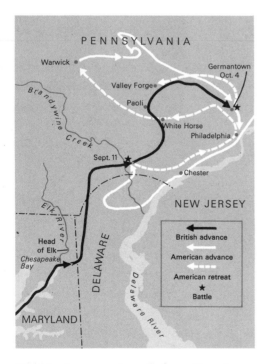

Washington moved south from New Jersey to counter Howe's landing in Maryland. After clashing at Brandywine and Germantown, the British occupied Philadelphia and the Patriots withdrew to Valley Forge.

to Chesapeake Bay, came ashore at Head of Elk, Maryland on August 25, and skirmished toward Philadelphia.

By this time, Washington had collected 11,000 men against Howe's 15,000. In a formal battle he was likely to be defeated. If he merely retreated he would keep his army safe. But in either case Philadelphia would fall to the British.

This would not mean final victory for Howe; he would not necessarily crush American resistance even by occupying every town from Maine to Georgia. But Congress would once more be homeless; Philadelphia was the largest city in America and its loss would—Washington saw—"strike . . . a damp" in American hearts.

So he risked battle with Howe, at Brandywine Creek near Wilmington, Delaware, on September 11. As on Long Island the Americans were outflanked and defeated. However, some troops under Nathanael Greene, sent by Washington to avert disaster, held on stubbornly until dusk. The army regrouped, still intact.

Washington and Howe were drawn up for another battle, but a heavy storm prevented them from fighting. On September 26 Howe, unopposed, entered Philadelphia. Yet the Continental Army was too near for him to relax entirely. There was another sharp fight at Germantown, several miles outside Philadelphia, on October 4.

The year had begun well for Washington, but his luck went against him

Washington, taking the offensive, attacked the British on the main Germantown road. The four-pronged attack (background), led by Generals Wayne and Sullivan, was delayed when a division of the American troops tried to rout out the redcoats from Chew House (right).

towards the end. Although he had done his best, the British were in Philadelphia, snug for the winter. The Americans had lost 2,000 men at Brandywine and Germantown, not to mention fifty slaughtered at Paoli in a surprise bayonet attack. Moreover, the local population seemed distressingly ready to welcome Howe's British and Hessian troops.

By contrast, Washington's weary, despondent battalions had to find themselves a winter encampment somewhere outside Philadelphia, to keep an eye on Howe. In the recent fighting the countryside had been stripped bare of food. What was left was being sold to the British

The place Washington chose was a bare, windswept plateau known as Valley Forge. Here "poor food—hard lodging—cold weather—fatigue —nasty clothes—nasty cookery" (as one of Washington's officers wrote) made existence almost unendurable. It was a bitter time, almost the worst of the whole war for the hard-pressed Commander in Chief.

5

FORGING A VICTORY

The tattered army at Valley Forge passes in review before Washington and his aides.

The winter of 1777–78 at Valley Forge was not entirely grim. By effort, huts were built to replace the leaky canvas tents of the initial weeks. Although food remained short, and clothing so inadequate that some of the soldiers looked like scarecrows, morale was surprisingly high.

One reason for the triumph over defeatism was that the General and his senior officers shared the hardship of their men instead of moving to more comfortable quarters. Another —even more important—was that one of the volunteer soldiers from Europe, Baron von Steuben, was an excellent instructor who taught the Continentals some lessons in drill. This was a

In this 1778 cartoon the brothers Howe doze at Philadelphia (background), as France, Holland, and Spain gleefully milk dry the cow of British commerce and America saws off its horns. The distraught Englishman at right is unable to rouse the sleeping British lion.

far more useful exercise than it might appear; in eighteenth-century warfare the movements of the parade ground formed the basis of an army's actual battle drill. To learn how to keep and change formation was much more than a ceremonial business; it could mean the difference between victory and defeat.

Another consolation to the hard-pressed Americans was that if Howe had made some progress, he had not made enough. He had used up a whole precious campaigning season to gain Philadelphia, but had failed to destroy Washington's army. The Loyalists Howe had counted on did not gather around his flag.

General Howe had failed because he had done nothing decisive enough to weaken American resistance. Gloomily, he measured his limited accomplishment against what he had expected—and sent in his resignation. Although he did not leave for home until May, 1778, he spent his last months doing almost nothing. First Gage, now Howe: Washington had outlasted two British commanders.

A third and more dazzling source of comfort for the Valley Forge Continentals was that Burgoyne's expedition from Canada had ended in disaster.

Burgoyne had reached and captured Fort Ticonderoga by early July,

86

1777. Thereafter, encumbered with too many wagons and taking the wrong roads through the wilderness, he had made slower and slower progress. He began to run short of food. And the militia, swarming around his column, were a constant worry. Near the town of Bennington on August 16, an enterprising group of Green Mountain Boys led by John Stark killed or captured a thousand of Burgoyne's men whom he had sent on a large-scale foraging raid into southern Vermont.

Suddenly Burgoyne was in serious trouble. St. Leger's diversionary British advance down the Mohawk Valley, expected to link up with him, was forced to turn back into Canada. Howe was too involved in Pennsylvania to help. Clinton advanced up the Hudson to Kingston in October but lost his nerve and returned to New York.

Horatio Gates, who had replaced Schuyler in the northern command, sat across Burgoyne's path with about 17,000 men—more than double the British strength.

Unwilling to retreat, Burgoyne got as far as Saratoga, only to find that he was almost encircled. Twice he tried to smash through, and failed. In mid-October he gave up.

Under the terms of the surrender agreement—the Convention of Saratoga—Burgoyne agreed to cease fighting; but in theory his British and German army had not really surrendered. The Convention guaranteed that they would be allowed to return home, minus their arms. Congress, however, rejected the Convention and treated Burgoyne's men as prisoners.

The northern army had shattered a British professional army; the men Burgoyne had lost were nearly impossible to replace. Back in 1775, there had been a good deal of doubt whether American amateurs could match European professionals. After 1778 there was little further doubt.

Still more important, the French were most impressed. For some time, through the agency of Benjamin Franklin and other Americans in Europe, they had been secretly supplying

After they were defeated at Saratoga, British troops lay down their arms in a formal surrender ceremony on October 17, 1777.

Washington, given the trappings of a European general in this French print, holds two important documents—the Declaration of Independence and the Treaty of Alliance.

make common cause with the United States. The alliance was to be an active one, with the aim of securing American "liberty, sovereignty, and independency, absolute and unlimited." In other words, France would go to war with England. Within the next couple of years half of Europe lined up against the sadly perplexed British government.

The men at Valley Forge heard this wonderful news at the beginning of May, 1778. Formed in ranks in the spring sunshine, they saluted the French with a salvo of artillery and warmed their insides with a special issue of rum. "I believe no event," wrote Washington, "was ever received with more heartfelt joy."

Although the prospects for the United States were now brighter after so much disappointment, the Commander in Chief was peculiarly disturbed. He had not sought his appointment, and he was still serving without pay and without leave of absence. He had not seen Mount Vernon for three whole years (and would not see it again for another three). He longed for its tranquil routines, and whenever he had leisure wrote to Lund Washington, his manager, to ask about crops and improvements.

Washington, of course, had no intention of giving up. But there were indications that others meant to force him out. The composition of Congress had greatly changed since Washington's unanimous appointment in 1775. Several of its members were

the Americans with arms and equipment. They wanted to see their old enemy, Britain, humiliated, and only hesitated to side openly with the colonists until they were certain the Americans could give a good account of themselves. The news of Saratoga was decisive.

In February, 1778, the jubilant Franklin was able to inform Congress that the French king had agreed to now openly critical of him. He had been overpraised, they said, and given too much power. America did not want another monarch. He was a dull, clumsy commander; what had he accomplished in comparison with the brilliant Gates? Or was he as good a soldier as Charles Lee, who had been exchanged for a British officer and come back to the Americans?

Some of Washington's officers—Alexander Hamilton, and the eager young French volunteer, the Marquis de Lafayette—were sure that there was an actual "cabal" or plot against him. Its aim, they believed, was to intrigue in Congress and put Horatio Gates in their Commander's place.

One private letter that came into Washington's hands seemed to suggest that the story was true. It had been written by Thomas Conway, another volunteer from abroad. Addressed to Gates, the letter praised him extravagantly and described Washington as a "weak General." Probably there was no organized plot. After all, as Conway later protested, Gates was a fine soldier and this was supposed to be a free country.

Nevertheless, if there *was* any sinister move afoot, it was soon squashed. Challenged to a duel by General John Cadwalder, Conway was badly hurt. Congress dismissed him from the service, and he returned to France—having the grace to apologize to Washington for his discourtesy. Gates was thereby reminded, if he needed a reminder, that for all the

General Horatio Gates, by C. W. Peale

freedom of action he had been allowed, Washington was still supreme commander of the American forces.

As for Charles Lee, his days of influence were almost over. In June, 1778, the British evacuated Philadelphia. Clinton, named to replace Howe, had decided to concentrate his regiments at New York, in case a French invasion fleet turned up there. As the redcoats tamely set out on the march toward New York, Washington left Valley Forge without regret and followed on Clinton's heels.

On June 28, a Sunday so broilingly hot that scores of men on both sides collapsed, the Continentals attacked a British column near Monmouth Court House, New Jersey.

Lee, in charge of the American vanguard, had not favored an attack, pressed it listlessly, and allowed his

CHICAGO HISTORICAL SOCIETY

An undaunted General Washington rides into the heat of battle at Monmouth Court House to rally the faltering Continental Army. Two veterans (left) carry a ragged captured British standard to their Commander. The medic at right attends a wounded American officer.

men to stream back in disorder when the British made a quick counterthrust. Riding up in fury, Washington reprimanded Lee (some accounts say he swore lustily) for throwing away a promising opportunity, and took charge of the situation himself. The Americans held.

Each side had suffered about 350 casualties when the fight was broken off and Clinton continued his march to the safety of New York. Lee, who sent in a contemptuous letter of complaint, was court-martialed for "insubordination" and for the rest of the war never held active command. Once more, George Washington had proved that he was master of the situation.

He needed all the support he could get, for the French alliance was to demand special gifts of tact, patience, and firmness. Among the blessings of French intervention (added to that of Spain which entered the coalition against Britain a year later) was the change in the balance of sea power. The British could no longer pick and choose their objectives; they now risked being caught by a powerful enemy fleet.

In fact, Clinton had reason to hurry back to defend New York City in the summer of 1778. A French fleet *was* on the way. If used together with Washington's army, which had grouped north of New York at White Plains by the end of July, the fleet could have bottled up Clinton.

Things did not work out so simply. The French, under the Comte d'Estaing, were unable to attack the British fleet which was anchored in waters too shallow for the French ships to enter. Instead they attempted to capture the British garrison holding Newport, Rhode Island, were driven off by a storm, and made for the West Indies.

John Sullivan, in charge of the American land force besieging Newport, was disgusted by the French admiral's action. Washington, however, realized that he could issue suggestions but not orders to allies, and in public had to be elaborately polite to the French.

The situation was tantalizing. The French had ships and soldiers, yet their support—at first—was ineffective. Possibly they were content to let the war in America drag on for a while. If it ended too quickly, the British would have resources to spare for the fighting that ranged across the globe—in the West Indies, in the English Channel and the North Sea, in the Mediterranean, and faraway in the Indian Ocean.

Thus it was that the French fleet dodged to and fro, never available at exactly the place and time that Washington wanted. It existed as a threat, a factor to make the British more inclined to hesitate before risking what Washington liked to call "a brilliant stroke."

And the war dragged on. Some Americans, as Washington had feared, were tending to relax their efforts, mistakenly thinking that the

AN ALLY FOR AMERICA

Even before the 1778 alliance, sympathetic Frenchmen were offering the United States their support.
The twenty-year-old Marquis de Lafayette (top left)
reached Philadelphia in July, 1777, was commissioned
a major general, and faithfully served the Patriot
cause through Yorktown. In 1780 the arrival of 5,000
French troops—like the elegantly attired regiments
above—under the Comte de Rochambeau (top center),
tipped the scales in America's favor. When the French
fleet drove British ships from Virginia's Cape Henry
(left) in September, 1781, thus isolating Cornwallis
at Yorktown, America's final triumph was ensured.

93

mere fact of the French alliance was sufficient to win victories.

The British, pouncing now and then, were still able to dominate the coastal areas. Late in 1778, they landed in Georgia and overran the state. A year and a half later—in one of his few bold endeavors—Clinton led an army to South Carolina by sea, overpowered the American defenses at Charleston, and took more than 5,000 prisoners.

Meanwhile, Washington's army, weak in numbers, had been unable to take the offensive after his success at Monmouth in June, 1778. The fighting became local and bitter: raids, ruses, guerrilla clashes, looting, and atrocities on both sides (though rather more on the British).

Congress too had become woefully weak. Although it had adopted a form of government, the Articles of Confederation, in late 1777, it could not take effect until ratified by the states— a process not completed until March, 1781. The individual states, in fact, often behaved as if they were semisovereign powers. To the few Americans with a truly continental vision, of whom Washington was one, the picture was dismally disappointing.

And the Commander in Chief still could not get enough regular soldiers. Worse, he could not even pay the ones he had. Martha, who joined him at the winter camp in Morristown, New Jersey for the early months of 1780, said that the atmosphere at headquarters was joyless: "the distress of the army," she noted, made her husband "so unhappy that it distressed me exceedingly."

The troops grumbled, and with each successive winter there were increasingly ominous signs that they were sick of soldiering under existing conditions. More and more men deserted. Although he stiffened discipline—flogging for major offenses, death for the worst offense of all (desertion in the face of the enemy)— Washington knew punishment was not the proper action.

When mutiny broke out among the Pennsylvania and New Jersey

LIBRARY OF CONGRESS

Caught spying disguised in civilian clothing, Major John André acknowledged his rank and was hanged in British uniform.

Continentals in January, 1781, he had to force them into submission, and try to convince them of what he could not himself really believe: that their arrears of pay would be promptly met.

His tenacity was a marvel, especially when others left the cause. Schuyler, Sullivan, and the tough Virginian Daniel Morgan, all went home in 1779. Washington's arrogant young aide, Alexander Hamilton, picked a quarrel when his harassed Commander spoke sharply to him and temporarily withdrew in 1781.

One of the worst shocks of the war came in September, 1780, when three

A 1780 French map shows West Point fortifications. At the promontory is Fort Clinton whose guns commanded the Hudson River.

New York militiamen halted a civilian who was trying to pass through their lines. Suspicious, they searched him and found papers that proved that he was a British officer, Major John André, just returned from a secret meeting with Benedict Arnold.

Arnold, one of Washington's bravest officers, had long felt his contributions to the cause at Quebec and Saratoga had been overlooked by Congress, and had entered into secret negotiations with the enemy in May, 1779. A year later he asked to be put in command of West Point, with the intention of betraying this vital Hudson River fortress to the British.

Sickened and angered by the treachery, Washington had André hanged as a spy. But Arnold escaped arrest, went over to the British, and for the rest of the war, as an enemy brigadier general, conducted raids on American communities—a brutal kind of warfare that made him even more hated by his former comrades.

"Traitors are the growth of every country," wrote the saddened General, "and in a revolution of the present nature, it is more to be wondered at, that the catalogue is so small than that there have been found a few."

Between apathy, mutiny, and treason, Washington could be forgiven for declaring, in April, 1781, that unless matters greatly improved, "we are at the end of our tether." Were the advantages of the French alliance a mere illusion? How delicious and how remote Mount Vernon

95

Nathaniel Greene, by C. W. Peale   *Daniel Morgan, by C. W. Peale*

seemed when the Commander in Chief asked his manager, "How many lambs have you had this spring? . . . Have you made any attempts to reclaim more Land for meadow? . . . . Are you going to repair the Pavement of the Piazza?" The pressing need was to repair the whole American war effort. In 1781, however, a break appeared in the clouds.

The British had abandoned major efforts in the North. Clinton remained in New York, and Washington had to stay within reach to watch him, but the main hopes of the British now focused on the South. After capturing Charleston in May, 1780, and extending their hold over Georgia, they had tried to convert the entire region into a Loyalist stronghold.

One French diplomat thought this was a long-term plan, and quite a shrewd one. If they lost the North, they might still keep the slave states

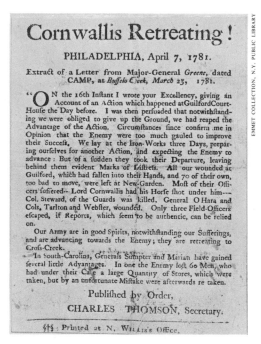

The headline of this broadside published in Philadelphia is optimistic, but misleading. Cornwallis was withdrawing not retreating.

under the British flag. In fact there was no such clear goal; the British were merely trying to hold together their North American empire.

Clinton left Cornwallis free to do what he could to extend control over the southern states, especially the Carolinas. Cornwallis, Washington's old opponent of Trenton and Princeton days, was a confident, energetic, and ruthless general. Some of his officers were even more ruthless.

The notorious cavalry leader Banastre Tarleton was as destructive as Sherman's Civil War "bummers," three quarters of a century later, and considerably more brutal. (A Carolina boy named Andrew Jackson never forgave Tarleton's men for their treatment of himself and his family. He would get his revenge against the British long afterward, at the Battle of New Orleans in 1815.)

At the outset Cornwallis's campaign of 1780-81 seemed to be going well for him. He routed an American force led by Gates at Camden, South Carolina in August, 1780. Among the killed was one of the ablest of the French volunteers, Baron de Kalb. Gates was ridiculed as a coward, and superseded by the sturdy ex-Quaker, General Nathanael Greene.

The struggle flamed across the South, the advantage shifting from one side to the other. Tarleton was beaten, largely by local militia under Daniel Morgan, at Cowpens, South Carolina on January 17, 1781. Thrusting north to the border of Virginia,

Cornwallis claimed a victory over Greene at Guilford Court House, North Carolina in March. But he was achieving nothing permanent. Every battle cost him men he could not replace. Far from being Loyalist in sentiment, district after district rose against him.

After withdrawing to Wilmington to receive reinforcements from a British fleet, Cornwallis left the Carolinas to invade Virginia. There were spectacular incidents, as when Tarleton's troopers almost captured Governor Thomas Jefferson at his home outside Charlottesville. Again, however, solid gains eluded the British. They failed to come to grips with small, quick-moving American forces led by Lafayette and Steuben.

Then Cornwallis decided to make for the coast, where the British fleet could come to his aid. He was still confident—too confident. An American observer, remembering Saratoga, predicted that Cornwallis would be "completely Burgoyned." Clinton, shrewd within his limits, foresaw the same result when he heard that in July Cornwallis had settled down at Yorktown, on the peninsula between the York and James rivers, expecting his army to be taken off by sea.

Nor was the move lost on Washington. With 5,000 Continentals and another 5,000 French troops under the Comte de Rochambeau at his disposal, he had been thinking about an attack on New York. The news of Cornwallis's dangerous maneuver and

A French engraving of the siege of Yorktown, with excessive patriotism, overemphasizes the French role in Cornwallis's final defeat. French officers on rearing horses command a

1842

battlefield crowded with more French than American troops. Yorktown is <u>conceived</u> as a medieval French walled city, and a huge French fleet chokes the waters close to shore.

word that Admiral de Grasse was coming north from the West Indies with an additional 3,000 Frenchmen, made Washington change his mind.

Leaving a token force north of New York to deceive Clinton, Washington and Rochambeau set out on August 21 on the long hot southward march to Virginia. In New Jersey they stopped long enough to build a dummy encampment, as if settling down for a siege of the city across the Hudson.

Not even the troops guessed the true destination of the combined armies. "General Washington . . . resolves and matures his great plans and designs under an impenetrable secrecy," an American army surgeon wrote in his journal, "and, while we repose the fullest confidence in our chief, our own opinions must be founded only on doubtful conjectures."

Not until September 2, when Washington was already at Philadelphia, did Clinton get wind of the move. By that time Washington's plan was well on schedule.

De Grasse's thirty ships reached the mouth of Chesapeake Bay just ahead of a British squadron and chased it off. Escape by sea was now closed to Cornwallis. Washington got word of de Grasse's timely arrival as his dusty columns filed into Maryland in early September. The Allied troops were loaded on transports, taken down Chesapeake Bay, and landed near Williamsburg, Virginia.

At last Washington could allow himself a few days at Mount Vernon. Then he was off again, along the familiar route to Williamsburg, just above Yorktown on the peninsula. With him came Alexander Hamilton, reconciled and eager for glory; and Jack Custis, to act as an aide-de-camp. This led to a personal tragedy, all the more painful when the rest of the operation was developing so beautifully. Jack caught "camp fever," rapidly weakened, and died. All the Commander in Chief could do was assure his widow that she and her infant children would be taken care of.

Otherwise the tragedy was Cornwallis's. With de Grasse's 3,000 men added to those picked up en route, Washington now commanded an army of 17,000, well supplied with guns and mortars. Cornwallis had less than half that number.

While the French ships sat downriver, the Allied troops rapidly and methodically laid siege to Yorktown. Artillery opened a bombardment, and hand-picked parties—one led by Hamilton—stormed the British outworks. On October 17, 1781, Cornwallis called for a truce, in despair—and on the fourth anniversary of that earlier British catastrophe at Saratoga. The defeated British general, excusing himself on grounds of illness,

A 1781 plan at right, shows the British trapped at Yorktown between the Franco-American land forces and the French fleet.

dodged the surrender ceremony two days later.

If ever a general deserved such a victory, it was George Washington; six long, grim years had passed since he had taken charge of the motley rebel force before Boston. In those years of frequent setbacks and few advances, he had made an army; he was now about to make a nation.

It was an extraordinary moment in history when the redcoats paraded to pile their arms and present Cornwallis's sword. As Washington sat his horse, flanked by his American and French associates, a British band struck up the ironical tune of "The World Turned Upside Down."

Further good news was coming in from the Carolinas and Georgia, where Greene was crushing what remained of enemy resistance, until by year's end only Charleston and Savannah were left in British hands.

Back in Great Britain, the defeat at Yorktown staggered and horrified the public. In conjunction with defeats in the West Indies and the Medi-

Unperturbed by cannon-balls exploding nearby, Washington and Lafayette observe the progress of their troops on the Yorktown battlefield. The infantry (left) leads the way to battle followed by the cavalry, in front of whom are several early casualties.

terranean, the reaction to this news finally brought down the government of Lord North, which had been responsible for the war. The administration that followed was ready to begin peace negotiations.

Clinton, like Gage and Howe, resigned and sailed for home to confront his critics and explain in his memoirs that whoever was to blame, it was not Sir Henry Clinton.

Life for the moment was pleasanter for Clinton's old antagonist. Washington went north by leisurely stages, not so much because he wanted to take things easy but because his countrymen were longing to celebrate. In Philadelphia, where he stayed for over three months, there was a succession of dinners and entertainments.

The French had grown to admire him almost as wholeheartedly as the Americans did. Although he could not speak their language, these aristocratic officers found him a polished gentleman, dignified, and yet easy in manner. Years of experience had given him an expert grasp of military affairs. His staff or "military family" was made up of efficient, cultivated young American officers. Any plainness in their style of living, which might in fact be caused by the inability of Congress to pay its army, was charitably explained as republican simplicity.

One French nobleman confessed that where he had "expected to see unkempt soldiers and officers without training . . . I saw a well-disciplined army presenting . . . the very image of order, reason, training and experience." Another, Chevalier Chastellux, commented on the precision of the Commander in Chief's bodyguard and on the "very fine horses belonging to the General Officers and their Aides de Camp. . . ."

They were not mistaken. Long association had bred a remarkable *esprit de corps* in Washington's camp. But this spirit could turn sour. His officers and men saw themselves as saviors of their country. They had suffered hardship and danger while others stayed in safety and grew rich.

One outcome of this dissatisfaction was a suggestion put to the Commander in Chief by certain officers, in May, 1782, that he assume "the title of King." Washington refused with crushing severity.

A second sign of unrest was the circulation of anonymous "Addresses" at his headquarters near Newburgh, New York in March, 1783, citing the Army's grievances and hinting that the Continentals should win justice by the display of force. He spoke to his officers, putting on spectacles to read his notes, with fatherly firmness: "Gentlemen, you must pardon me. I have grown gray in your service and now find myself growing blind."

The army should remember that it was the country's servant, not its master, he said. Washington would be no party to plots and threats. There

The painting of Washington's December 4, 1783, farewell to his officers is by Alonzo Chappel.

must be no more of these anonymous petitions. The ringleaders, whoever they were, were wise enough to learn the lesson he read them.

At his urging, Congress promised back pay to the soldiers. But the pay-chests were still empty, and most of his long-suffering Continentals set off for their homes with empty pockets when the war was over.

On November 30, 1782, the four American commissioners in Europe—Benjamin Franklin, John Adams, John Jay, and Henry Laurens—had signed provisional articles of peace with the British. Not until September 3, 1783, at Paris, was the definitive formal peace treaty signed. But the American negotiators in Paris had won a great diplomatic victory: American independence was recognized. And the boundaries of the new nation were to stretch from the Atlantic to the Mississippi, and from Maine and the Great Lakes to the frontier of Spanish Florida.

At long last the Commander could follow his men on the homeward path, eight and a half years after he staked his life and his "sacred honor" on the perilous cause of American liberty. Normally a stern man on public occasions, he was so moving when he said good-bye to his officers at Fraunces' Tavern in New York that several of them wept openly. Not trusting himself to speak, he silently embraced them one by one.

As he journeyed south on his last assignment, Washington was cheered

MANUSCRIPT DIVISION, LIBRARY OF CONGRESS

Washington's last official document as Commander in Chief was the Farewell Orders to the Armies published on November 2, 1783. The first and last pages are shown above.

at every stop. Guns boomed out and church bells rang. At Annapolis, Maryland, where Congress was in session, in a brief emotional ceremony he handed back "with satisfaction" the commission he had accepted "with diffidence." No one who was present would ever forget the scene.

Then he slipped away, a free man in more senses than one, hurrying to reach Mount Vernon and Martha's welcome by Christmas Eve, 1783.

6

CITIZEN IN RETIREMENT

Shortly after his retirement to Mount Vernon at the end of 1783, George Washington described himself as "a private citizen of America, on the banks of the Potomac . . . under my own Vine and my own Fig-tree, free from the bustle of a camp and the intrigues of a court." He did not intend to be burdened with any further public cares. "I am not only retired from all public employments, but I am retiring within myself." He would live as a simple farmer, following what he told a fellow Virginian was "the most delectable" of all the ways to earn a living.

Washington was just past fifty years old when he resigned his commission. He had not had a single illness while he was Commander in Chief—a remarkable record, and in sharp contrast with his days of soldiering for Virginia when he had had several long intervals of disabling sickness. He struck those who met him

Once again a Virginia squire, Washington with Martha on his arm strolls across the bowling green in front of Mount Vernon.

as still vigorous and lithe. He and Martha had no children of their own, and hers were both dead. They adopted two of Jackie Custis's little children, a boy and a girl, whose cheerful presence made Mount Vernon once again seem like a young household.

And yet, especially at first, George Washington felt old. Once the strain of his enormous responsibility was lifted he realized how tired he was. At this period his teeth were causing him pain. Before long he had them all removed. The false teeth carved for him of ivory and set in a heavy metal frame were clumsy to wear, made public speeches even more of an ordeal, and fixed his jaw in the unnaturally rigid lines reflected in the familiar portraits done by Gilbert Stuart.

The wartime deaths of Jack Custis and many another gay young officer weighed heavily on his mind. In the next few years several men close to him died—including the staunchest among his wartime lieutenants Nathanael Greene, and his favorite brother John Augustine.

No wonder then that he talked so

wistfully, in the familiar Biblical phrase, of sitting quietly under his vine and his fig tree. He ordered a quantity of books in the hope of leisure for reading. Some of them were travel books; indeed, his ardent friend the Marquis de Lafayette, now back in France, was begging him to come and visit. He resumed his diary, which he had abandoned for most of the war years.

His dream of undisturbed peace was soon shattered. Washington discovered that his finances were in poor shape. His generous gesture of serving without pay cost him dearly; Mount Vernon and his other plantations were run down, and squatters had occupied his western holdings. Like many of his countrymen he was "land-poor," he had little actual cash, and the "Continentals" (paper currency) were disastrously depreciated.

Even if he had not wished to, Washington had to stir himself to put his affairs in order. Before long he was absorbed in the management of the Mount Vernon farms. He bought fertilizer to improve the depleted soil, and experimented with new seeds and fresh crops. He built a new barn on the latest model, and imported an English farm manager trained in scientific agriculture.

The house itself was not yet in the elegant condition it presents to visitors today. The chimneys needed repair, and the piazza was still to be paved. At this time he started to build a new room, the "banquet hall,"

partly to accommodate an increasing number of guests. He wrote dozens of letters about wallpaper, bookshelves, Venetian blinds, a new greenhouse, a new deer park, and new lawns and paths. He laid out a fruit garden, and redesigned his icehouse to preserve food during the summer months.

But the world outside refused to leave him to his peaceful pursuits. Throughout America and Europe

Lafayette, visiting Mount Vernon in 1784, talks to Washington in a tranquil setting that includes Martha and her grandchildren.

Washington was renowned as the modern Cincinnatus, an allusion to the early Roman patriot who had left his farm to save his country in wartime crisis, and who then, instead of seizing power as he could have, returned to his plow. It was an appro-priate comparison. But if the Roman Cincinnatus was allowed to enjoy his retirement, the American one was not.

Every traveler in the United States was anxious to make George Washington's acquaintance. They descended on Mount Vernon in an unceasing stream. The rule of Virginia hospitality and his own courtesy made them welcome. As late as June, 1785, he noted in his diary: "Dined with only Mrs. Washington, which I believe is the first instance of it since my retirement from public life."

There was little privacy at Mount Vernon. One night, after the Washingtons and several guests had already gone to bed, the General was awakened to greet four more visitors—the famous French sculptor Jean Houdon and his three assistants, who had come to do a portrait bust. While Houdon's party was still at Mount Vernon, workmen were hammering shingles on the roof; and inside the house there was the added noise and excitement of a wedding between a nephew of George's and a niece of Martha's.

Those who could not visit wrote to him. During the war a succession of efficient young men had acted as his secretaries. From 1783 to 1786, however, he was unable to find a suitable secretary of his own. Yet in those years, as he complained in a letter to a friend, he was busier than before:

. . . at no period of the war have I been obliged to write half as much as I do now. . . . What with letters . . . from foreigners. Enquiries after Dick, Tom, and Harry, who *may have been* . . . in the Continental service . . . Introductions; applications for copies of Papers; references of a thousand old matters . . . which must receive an answer of some kind, deprive me of my usual exercise; and without relief, may be injurious to me as I already begin to feel the weight, the oppression of it in my head.

Fort Robertdeau, pictured in 1787, was a rough hewed outpost in sparsely populated western Pennsylvania—still looked upon as frontier-territory by newly independent Americans.

Eventually order was brought to the chaotic situation, when he found an excellent and loyal secretary, Tobias Lear. Washington could not help but be flattered by the gifts and enthusiastic letters that flowed in from admirers. He was able to spend more time in his "usual exercise" of horseback riding, either to inspect his farms or in fox hunting. The farms grew to six in number, and the Mount Vernon colony of slaves to more than two hundred.

As the conduct of his affairs was regulated, he was also able to turn his attention further afield. In 1784, with his nephew Bushrod Washington and a surgeon, Dr. James Craik, Washington set out on a western journey. They traveled past Fort Necessity and along the road Braddock had hacked out thirty years earlier, to look at Washington's Virginia bounty lands. The expedition was both disturbing and exciting.

The squatters on his western land were surly and arrogant (he eventually tried to evict them). Their mood and that of other frontiersmen was alarmingly narrow. The United States was to them a remote, almost alien country. So indeed was Virginia. In these years Virginia, Connecticut, and other states with huge western land claims were one by one surrendering their millions of frontier acres to the national government. But for the moment no effective authority replaced them.

In the North Carolina back-country the separate state of "Franklin" emerged, with only the loosest ties to the original thirteen states. Unless a firm hand were laid upon such communities, they might stay outside the United States. Spanish intrigue, directed from Florida and Louisiana, encouraged such separation. Farther north, the British were still in possession of their fur-trading posts. They admitted that the posts were on American soil, but excused themselves with the counterargument that the Americans had not honored their side of the peace treaty. Congress was unable to persuade the states to pay old debts to English creditors, return confiscated property to Loyalists, and pledge to avoid further reprisals.

If these problems began to alarm Washington, he saw a partial answer in schemes to improve communications with the West. In this way the frontiersmen would be drawn into association with the Union instead of going their own way. Western lands would rise in value; trade would be profitable.

The idea was not new to Washington: it merely seemed more urgent. Years before the Revolutionary War he had been eager to develop his own river, the Potomac, which was navigable for quite a long way upstream. If a small canal were dug around the Great Falls of the Potomac, and a portage organized to the headwaters of the Ohio tributaries, there might be a dramatic increase in commerce. He filled pages of his diary

MOUNT VERNON ENSHRINED

The dedication of a small group of women who formed the Mount Vernon Ladies Association in 1858 saved the decaying home of President Washington for posterity. In order to restore the mansion to its 1799 appearance, they have collected original furnishings and added authentic reproductions. The second-floor bedroom (left) is dominated by the oversize four-poster in which the General died; his elegant secretary-desk (right) stands in the library. From the outside kitchen (below), food was taken to the family dining room (opposite, below) where the silver tea urn (far left) with the Custis coat of arms was used.

with arguments concerning the advantages of his proposals.

Moving swiftly—in part because he wanted a head start over rival schemes, including one for the development of the James River—Washington organized a Potomac River company. Virginia and Maryland shared rights to the river; he persuaded them to support his plan, and commissioners from both states met at Mount Vernon in the spring of 1785. It was suggested that Virginia and Maryland ought to meet annually to discuss ways of cooperating. In fact there were so many overlapping interests that the Virginia legislature helped to promote a convention at Annapolis in September, 1786, to which all thirteen states were invited —though only five including Virginia came.

The delegates at Annapolis made plans for another convention, to be held the following year at Philadelphia. This meeting was a larger affair, presided over by General Washington: and before adjourning the delegates were to draw up an entirely new constitution to replace the inadequate Articles of Confederation.

In the meantime, Washington's interests in western expansion were leading him naturally toward fresh involvement in public life. As Commander in Chief he had shed nearly all his Virginia localism. In peace, he continued to think on a continental scale. Even more than Congress, Washington, as the architect of vic-

tory in the Revolutionary War, symbolized the United States.

One of the major lessons Washington had learned from the war was that it could have been fought more effectively, more quickly, and less expensively if the central government had been stronger. A good many times during the war the Commander in Chief had written to governors of states to try and convince them of the dangers of "contracted ideas, local pursuits and absurd jealousy." He had expanded his views in a circular sent to all the states in June, 1783, which he later described to John Jay as his "last legacy." America could only prosper, he said in the circular, as "an indissoluble Union of the States under One Federal Head."

Nevertheless he was reluctant after 1783 to be active in schemes to alter the Government of the United States. The Articles of Confederation left the individual states free to decide most things for themselves. Anything more powerful in the way of a central government smacked too much of the despotisms of the Old World. Yet he preferred to leave the task of drawing up a new constitution to men like John Adams or his young Virginia colleague James Madison. As for agitation to change the Articles, this could only be done with the unanimous consent of the states, and he knew from wartime experience how hard it was, in Benjamin Franklin's phrase, to "make thirteen clocks strike as one."

An 1800 drawing conveys the natural beauty of the Potomac's Great Falls, but omits a new canal first suggested by Washington.

Above all, perhaps Washington was tired of having to take the lead. Whenever he agreed to be chairman or president of something, he only added to his worries. Thus he had agreed to preside over an ex-officers' group known as the Society of the Cincinnati. Because it was confined to officers, and was to be hereditary, it was hotly attacked as a sinister aristocratic movement. He wished he had never been involved with the Cincinnati and pleaded ill-health as an excuse for not attending the Society's next meeting, which was to take place at Philadelphia in May, 1787—at the same time as the meeting of all the states. But when Virginia chose him as a delegate to the Constitutional Convention, he was forced once more to accept the call of duty.

John Jay (Secretary of Foreign Affairs under the Articles) and others had been active in arguing that a new government was essential. They knew that nothing could be done without the great General's support. So they

115

wrote to him again and again to point out America's present weaknesses. The states were quarreling with one another. Britain and Spain were openly contemptuous. There was no American Army to defend the nation's interests, except for a handful of men looking after rusty equipment at West Point.

Gradually Washington became convinced that his correspondents were right. What finally helped to persuade him that the Confederation was "a rope of sand" was an upheaval in western Massachusetts in the fall of 1786. During the war years American farmers had received high prices for their produce. Now they were feeling the pinch of low prices, unusable currency, and heavier taxes than they were used to. Farmers everywhere grumbled. Those in inland Massachusetts, resenting their state government, staged a small rebellion under the leadership of a veteran of Bunker Hill, Captain Daniel Shays. The state militia had to be called out, and there was some shooting.

Washington was appalled at this evidence of disorder. "We are fast verging to anarchy and confusion!" he exclaimed to James Madison. "Are your people getting mad?" he wrote to an acquaintance in Massachusetts. "What is the cause of all this? When and how is it to end?"

Once Washington made up his mind he acted, knowing that his dream of peace and quiet at Mount Vernon was again receding. Despite his embarrassment over the Cincinnati, despite twinges of rheumatism, despite the sadness of leaving Martha again, he took the road to Philadelphia, much as he had done more than twenty years earlier, to attend another convention with fateful consequences.

This time also he perhaps did not foresee how far-reaching the consequences might be. All he knew was that Congress had approved the Convention; that the meeting would consider revisions to the Articles of Confederation; and that it was likely to be fairly well attended. (As it happened, Patrick Henry refused to join the Virginia delegation, saying he "smelt a rat;" New Hampshire's delegates did not arrive until late July; and Rhode Island was not represented at all.)

He might also have guessed that, because of his extraordinary prestige, he would be elected to preside over the Convention.

When he arrived in Philadelphia in his family coach on May 13 it was like earlier days: bells rang out and guns boomed a salute. No less than thirty of the fifty-five delegates had served as officers in the militia or the Continental Army. Four of them, including Alexander Hamilton—now a busy New York lawyer, married to the daughter of Philip Schuyler—had been on Washington's own staff. They were as a whole talented, educated, civic-minded—and extremely talkative. At the outset they agreed to meet in secret, and to draft a new constitution instead of tinkering with the old one.

For a while they seemed unable to agree on much else. Their debates were so intricate and so heated that at one stage Washington wrote he regretted "having had any agency in the business." The large states, with whom Washington as a Virginian sided, wanted representatives to be allotted according to population. The small states understandably preferred the existing arrangement in which each state had an equal voice. There was hostility to a strong executive,

which Washington also had favored.

At moments the Convention was near deadlock. Hamilton's notions were rejected by the other New York delegates. Outside Independence Hall the air had grown hot and humid, when the Convention—exhausted by weeks of continuous argument—took a ten-day recess late in July. Washington used the opportunity to visit old haunts at Valley Forge and Trenton.

Back in session on August 6, he and the others gradually thrashed out compromises. The charm of white-haired Benjamin Franklin, past eighty but still resourceful, and the shrewdness of James Madison helped. Some delegates, it is true, were so displeased that they walked out; some like George Mason stayed to the end, but refused to sign the finished document.

A working majority of the delegates stuck to the task, however, until in early September a Committee on Style could get down to the final business of composing the Constitution. There would be a President, indirectly elected for a four-year term by an electoral college chosen by the people; a Senate, two members from each state, indirectly elected by state legislatures for six-year terms; and a House of Representatives, popularly elected for two-year terms, the number from each state to vary with its population.

An intricate system of "checks and balances" among the President and each of the two houses would ensure that no branch of government would

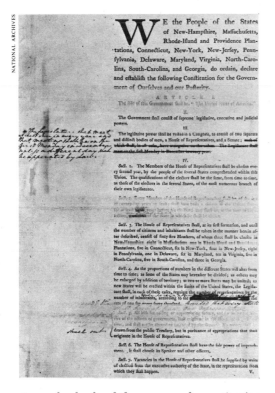

An early draft of the proposed constitution was subject to revision. Washington's copy had penned corrections on the first page.

have too much power over the others. An independent Federal judiciary would play its part in balancing authority. Although the new Government would be a much stronger one than the Confederation, a reasonable amount of sovereignty remained with the individual states, according to the theory of "Federal" government.

The Constitution fitted in with Washington's conviction, the result of years of painful experience, that America could not become a real nation until it had an effective central authority—"an indissoluble Union of the States," to repeat his words of 1783, "under One Federal Head." After the long labors of the summer

Washington presides over the final day's work of the delegates to the 1787 Convention —the signing of the Constitution. In Thomas Rossiter's painting of the historic ceremony, Washington is seated on a dais. Behind him is a tapestry featuring a sunburst design.

Mount Vernon looked handsomer than ever to him that fall of 1787. A dove of peace, made of iron, was fixed to the cupola as a weathervane. Perhaps it was a symbol.

But he could not rest easy. The Constitution had still to be ratified by at least nine of the states. There was a great deal of opposition, dragging on throughout the winter and spring. Close argument and maneuver went on in state conventions. It was necessary to promise several of the states that the Constitution would be amended to include a "Bill of Rights," similar to the guarantees of individual liberties in most of the Revolutionary state constitutions. Not until June, 1788, when New Hampshire ratified, was the Constitution accepted.

Washington, his own reputation at stake, had worried over the fate of the Constitution. Now he had another worry. Every sign pointed to him as the first President under the new instrument of Government. Everyone who offered a toast or made a speech at July 4 celebrations mentioned his name. One typical effort at Wilmington, Delaware, was: "Farmer Washington—May he like a second Cincinnatus, be called from the plow to rule a great people." As early as January, 1788 Lafayette had begged him "not to deny your acceptance of the office of President for the first years. You only can settle that political machine . . ."

Washington realized that this was probably true. There *was* no other candidate. But the task was enough to daunt any man. "I should," he said, "consider myself as entering upon an unexplored field, enveloped on every side with clouds and darkness." In April, 1789, while he waited at Mount Vernon for the inevitable summons, he poured out his anguish in a letter to his old army friend, Henry Knox:

. . . my movements to the chair of Government will be accompanied by feelings not unlike those of a culprit . . . going to the place of his execution: so unwilling am I, in the evening of a life nearly consumed in public cares, to quit a peaceful abode for an Ocean of difficulties. . . . I am embarking the voice of my Countrymen and a good name of my own, on this voyage, but what returns will be made for them, Heaven alone can foretell.

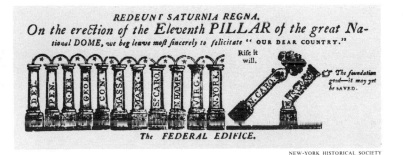

REDEUNT SATURNIA REGNA.
On the erection of the Eleventh PILLAR of the great National DOME, we beg leave most sincerely to felicitate " OUR DEAR COUNTRY."

Rise it will.

The foundation good—it may yet be SAVED.

The FEDERAL EDIFICE.

In a wry 1788 cartoon on Constitutional ratification, eleven columns (states) are in place, but the other two appear somewhat unsteady.

7

The summons arrived in mid-April, 1789, by special messenger. General Washington was the unanimous choice of the electors, with John Adams of Massachusetts selected as his Vice-President. The new Congress was assembled in New York, which for the time being would serve as the nation's capital, to await his arrival.

Whatever his misgivings, Washington responded promptly. Two days after the messenger had reached Mount Vernon, the President-elect said goodbye to Martha, who was to join him in a few weeks, and set out for New York. He was cheered and feted all along the route. For the final stage he was brought by water in an elegant sailing barge to the foot of Wall Street. Every ship and boat lying off Manhattan paid tribute with flags and salutes of cannon. It was a gay and yet solemn scene.

The President-elect was soon ensconced in a temporary home on Cherry Street, near what is now the Manhattan end of Brooklyn Bridge. There was not an entire break with

The grateful citizens of Trenton, scene of Washington's major war triumph, greet the President-elect en route to New York City.

PRESIDENT

Within the second-story portico of Federal Hall, overlooking Wall Street, Washington took the oath of office. At the end of the street stands Trinity Church, later rebuilt.

the past. His secretary, Tobias Lear, was waiting at Cherry Street, and had engaged as household steward the excellent cook Sam Fraunces, a West Indian at whose tavern Washington had held the farewell session with his officers six years before. Two old wartime companions, David Humphreys and Major William Jackson, joined him as secretaries. Many Congressmen were long-time acquaintances.

When Washington took the oath of office on April 30, outside Federal Hall, the occasion was immensely impressive. Tall and dignified, his hair powdered and a dress-sword at his side, Washington had—in the words of the French Minister—"the soul, look and figure of a hero." His fellow countrymen could note also with approval the President's patriotic gesture of wearing a brown suit made of cloth woven in Connecticut.

Although his inaugural address was delivered a little awkwardly, its phrases were well put and his very modesty delighted the vast crowd. Things were beginning well, yet much was still uncertain. Rhode Island and North Carolina had refused to ratify the Constitution and so were not yet in the Union. The states were burdened with debt. The British had not sent a diplomatic representative. But Americans had enormous confidence in Washington. They liked his appeal for unity, his apology for his own "inferior endowments," and his declaration that he did not wish to be paid a salary. (This wish was set aside: Congress voted the President an annual salary of $25,000.)

Little by little the patterns of government began to take shape. It was a slow business, involving such endless discussion in Congress that one of its members, James Madison of Virginia, grumbled: "We are in a wilderness without a single footstep to guide us."

However, there were advantages in going slowly, and feeling the way. The executive departments established by the Continental Congress—Foreign Affairs, War, Treasury, and Post Office—still more or less functioned. In the first months, places were filled and vital precedents were established. Fat Henry Knox, who had served as Washington's artillery officer, remained as Secretary of War. Foreign Affairs were to be the province of the new Department of State, headed by the brilliant Virginian Thomas Jefferson. The equally brilliant New Yorker, Alexander Hamilton, was made Secretary of the Treasury. John Jay, also of New York, became the first Chief Justice of the Supreme Court. Edmund Randolph of Virginia, who had somewhat disapproved of the 1787 Constitution, was won over by being given the post of Attorney General. Samuel Osgood of Massachusetts, a former member of the Treasury Board, became Postmaster General.

By later standards, government functioned on a small scale. The Postmaster General shared a room with one clerk, who sorted out the mail in front of him. Knox directed an army

The President and several members of the cabinet catch up on editorial opinion. Jefferson, Hamilton, and Washington (standing, left to right) listen intently while Henry Knox reads an article from the newspaper.

of only a few hundred men. There was no Navy Department, nor departments of Labor, Commerce, and the like destined for future years. There were a mere twenty-two Senators, and fifty-nine Representatives.

Yet all the members of the new government realized that decisions taken now would affect the whole shape of the future. So behavior was apt to be cautious and stiff. For the President there was a real problem of social style. He was head of state, and a good deal of official formality was expected of him. On the other hand, too much formality and display would lay him open to criticism that he was too much like a European monarch. Congress had already shown its sensitivity to this situation by deciding that he should be addressed not in any high-flown way (such as "His Mighti-

124

In a nineteenth-century painting of one of "Lady Washington's" receptions, the hostess (on dais at left) presides over her illustrious guests. John Jay, John Adams, and Alexander Hamilton are on her right. To her left are Thomas Jefferson (under the lady's portrait) and the President. Mrs. John Jay stands in full profile with the ladies grouped in the foreground.

ness" or "His Highness") but simply as "President of the United States"— in short, Mr. President.

Washington's compromise was probably the right one for the time. On Tuesday afternoons there would be official "levees" at his house. An American who attended one of these rather frigid occasions described how the President, dressed in black velvet, wore gloves and carried a cocked hat.

He bowed to visitors as they were presented but shook hands with none, not even with his personal friends. In other words, he was acting as the ceremonial head of government.

A more relaxed atmosphere marked the regular Friday evenings at which Martha Washington held open house for callers. Although some referred to her as "Lady Washington," she herself remained a cheerful and relaxed hostess. The President would put in an appearance and sometimes join in the lighthearted conversation.

In between these extremes came the Thursday afternoon dinners at which the Washingtons entertained government officials, foreign diplomats, and members of Congress. Most of the guests were awed by the President. According to William Maclay, a somewhat pugnacious Senator from Pennsylvania, no one quite knew how to behave. They waited for the President to speak, and he usually was not in a gay mood. But Abigail Adams, wife of the Vice-President, was charmed by Washington's stately manner and by the little courtesies he showed. At dinner he plucked the sugarplums from a cake and asked Abigail to take them for her grandson.

Still fond of the theater, the Washingtons also often took a private box and invited several guests to join them at a performance. On Sunday mornings they were seen at church; for the rest of the day, as the President often noted in his diary, he was busy with private affairs—writing letters about Mount Vernon and his other estates.

Time not taken up with official business was eaten up by other engagements—for example, having his portrait painted at the earnest request of Harvard College, or of some other institution. In February, 1790, he moved to a larger house on Broadway, which had room for fourteen white servants and seven slaves from Mount Vernon. Even so he felt cramped. In need of physical exercise, he rode out each morning for a couple of hours on his white horse, or drove in a coach with Martha and the Custis children.

Longer trips were sometimes possible. Anxious to examine the state of the Union for himself, he left New York in October, 1789, for a month's tour of New England. The following August he paid a special visit to Rhode Island, which in the meantime had entered the Union. The President was even able to spend most of the fall at Mount Vernon. In the spring of 1791, he made an extensive tour of the South —nearly 1,900 miles of travel, speechmaking, and handshaking.

What he saw on these tours reassured him. The United States was prosperous, he himself was enormously popular, and the Constitution was now accepted by almost everyone —especially since Congress had added the Bill of Rights. Provision was being made for a new, permanent seat of government. In September, 1790, the Federal Government shifted to Philadelphia, to stay there for ten years. Plans were under way for the building of a brand-new "Federal City" near Georgetown on the Potomac, which would be only a few easy miles from Mount Vernon.

Two things worried George Washington. One was his own health. The strain of office told upon him. In June, 1789, a painful swelling on his left hip —variously described as a "tumor" and as a "malignant carbuncle"—so reduced his vitality that he and others

Philadelphia's busy wharves are the subject of this engraving by William Birch. The new Federal Capital was America's commercial and cultural center as well as its largest city.

thought he might die. He was confined to his house for six weeks; at the worst period chains were stretched across the road outside to divert the noisy traffic. A year later he had a severe attack of pneumonia, with a near-fatal relapse. Senator Maclay noted in his diary:

"Called to see the President. Every eye full of tears. His life despaired of."

Washington was still a strong man. He recovered and was able to go fishing with Thomas Jefferson to recuperate. But he felt less vigorous than he liked, and in 1791 he was troubled by

127

another tumor. Possibly too he was becoming deaf. Although he never spoke of it to his associates, it may account for the apparent coldness of manner that Maclay and others criticized. He began to look forward to retirement at the end of his four-year term. Pondering the prospect, he asked James Madison to jot down some ideas for a farewell address.

Washington's second, larger worry was that there were beginning to be ominous signs of disunity in the young nation. Antagonisms developed between those who favored a strong Federal Government and those who wanted a weak one; some groups believed power should be in agrarian hands, while others took the view that it should rest with the business interests; and, in addition, there were those who offered great resistance to taxes.

If retirement seemed more and more alluring, it began to seem less and less feasible. Madison told him that the Government was in danger unless he stayed in office four more years, to give "tone and firmness" to public affairs. Without his guiding hand, the United States could still col-

The royal family of France fled, on August 10, 1792, from the mobs attacking their palace and placed themselves under the protection of the Legislative Assembly. Seated behind a screened reporter's box (right), the king and queen are confronted by menacing crowds.

lapse into anarchy, or turn into a monarchy. Jefferson began to argue along the same lines: "North and South will hang together if they have you to hang on." So, for many of the same reasons, pleaded Alexander Hamilton.

Washington feared that they were right. He also knew that the members of what men were beginning to call the "Cabinet" were in bitter disagreement with one another. And the disagreement was starting to produce an alignment along party and sectional lines, which he and the Founding Fathers had neither intended nor wanted.

The British example suggested that parties were corrupt and selfish—rival groups manipulating government for their own purposes. The French example was even more alarming: the Revolution which had broken out in Paris in 1789 was growing more violent. In 1792 and 1793 Washington watched in dismay while France was plunged into the "Reign of Terror," and the French king and queen went to the guillotine.

At home controversy began with the proposals of Treasury Secretary Hamilton. Clever, magnetic, confident, and ambitious, Hamilton had firm views on what should be done to save America. The Federal Government must be decisively stronger than the state governments. It must be controlled by sharp-witted, hard-headed, well-connected men such as himself: people of education, wealth, and in-fluence. If this powerful minority believed in the United States, they could make the country a going concern.

How could the allegiance of the rich and well-placed best be guaranteed? By putting America's finances on a sound basis, and by giving men of property a financial stake in the nation's affairs. In his famous reports of 1790 and 1791, Hamilton recommended a national bank; the raising of revenue through import duties and excises; and the assumption by the Federal Government of all outstanding debts, incurred by Congress *and* by the individual states. The United States would borrow to pay these old debts and the new national debt would be paid off by degrees.

Differences of opinion about the future development of America were bound to occur, and Hamilton's schemes were hotly opposed, by Jefferson in the cabinet and by Madison and others in Congress. They believed that Hamilton saw himself as a sort of British Prime Minister, and that he meant to turn America into another aristocracy, with power concentrated in the central Government and in the hands of the rich city-dwellers of the Northeast. Their own vision was of a decentralized nation of small communities in which no one was either rich or poor, and in which the Federal Government's powers were strictly limited.

Hamilton got most of what he wanted, and in the long run he may have been more correct than his op-

ponents. But his victories were bought at a price. He hastened the division of politically minded Americans into two hostile camps: the Federalists, who generally supported Hamilton, and the Anti-Federalists or Democratic Republicans (much later known simply as Democrats), who preferred the views of Jefferson and Madison.

By 1792 Washington came to realize that he must endure four more

Alexander Hamilton by John Trumbull

Jefferson is attacked for his Francophile sentiments in this pro-Federalist cartoon. Washington, driving the Federal chariot, leads his troops against the French "cannibals" invading the American shore; Jefferson (far right) tries to "stop de wheels of de gouvernement."

130

years in office to maintain the balance of power. As President he must try to stand above the conflict, taking sides with neither group. The situation was all the more difficult because Hamilton and Jefferson, his chief executive heads, actively encouraged two rival newspapers in which the controversy was ferociously argued. Hamilton added to Jefferson's problems as Secretary of State by meddling, and by supplying confidential information to British diplomats. In his own eyes, he acted for the best, though he came close to what we would now call treasonable behavior. Jefferson, while not quite so devious, was not always entirely candid himself.

Somehow Washington had to hold the two men and their rival factions in check. His own conduct was above suspicion. If we compare his correspondence during these years with that of Hamilton and Jefferson, he is easily the most impressive figure. He was not as learned or perhaps as brilliant as either man, and was forced to defer to Hamilton on economic questions. He was less subtle and ingenious; but he had more stability, more common sense, and a wider understanding of America's needs.

Yet at the time Washington was sadly perplexed. He urged Hamilton and Jefferson to settle their differences for the general good, but neither man was prepared to yield an inch. Reluctantly he allowed himself to be nominated and elected once more. On March 4, 1793, he and Vice-President

Votes.	George Washington	John Adams	George Clinton	Thomas Jefferson	Aaron Burr
New-Hampshire,	6	6			
Massachusetts,	16	16			
Rhode-Island,	4	4			
Connecticut,	9	9			
Vermont,	3	3			
New-York,	12		12		
New-Jersey,	7	7			
Pennsylvania,	15	14	1		
Delaware,	3	3			
Maryland,	8	8			
Virginia,	21		21		
Kentucky,	4			4	
North-Carolina,	12		12		
South-Carolina,	8	7			1
Georgia,	4		4		
	132	77	50	4	1

The Senate Journal of February 13, 1793, recorded Washington as the Electoral College's unanimous choice for a second term. The vote for Vice-President was divided.

John Adams were inaugurated for a second term.

That year the full force of the French Revolution began to be felt. In Europe, general war had broken out with France pitted against England—a struggle that was to last for the rest of Washington's life and beyond. Federalists and Democratic-Republicans were soon taking sides in the European contest.

The "Anglomen" of Hamilton's camp saw England as the hero and the struggle as one between religion and atheism, law and lawlessness. The

"Gallomen" of Jefferson's persuasion insisted that France was still America's true friend, Britain still the real enemy. Passions ran high. And the war between Britain and France presented the President with an urgent problem: what was America's declared policy to be?

Jefferson vigorously argued that France and the United States were still formal allies, under the Treaty of 1778, and friends in a wider sense. Each had made a revolution, and become a republic: they stood for the future, against the encrusted conservatism of wicked old Europe. Not so, said Hamilton: England was America's close partner in transatlantic trade. A common heritage of language and customs coupled with a mutual respect for law and order made it unthinkable that Americans should join forces with a blood-soaked France against England.

In fact neither side was proposing that the United States should go to war. The issue turned on the delicate matter of what sort of neutrality ought to be maintained.

Washington was certain that, as a broad policy, America must be genuinely, impartially neutral—and on April 22, 1793, he issued a proclamation to that effect. One or two resultant problems solved themselves.

The new French Minister to America, Edmond Charles Genêt, behaved so rashly that even Jefferson had to agree with the President when he demanded the Frenchman's recall.

Washington, appearing again in the role of Commander in Chief, reviews at Fort Cumberland the troops which were being sent to suppress the 1794 Whiskey Rebellion in Pennsylvania.

Genêt had acted as though the United States was a sort of revolutionary province of France, instead of being an independent nation. He had ordered several privateers from Charleston to seize British ships in United States waters, and had made plans to recruit Americans for an attack on Spanish Louisiana.

There were domestic achievements to offset the international crisis. Despite the touchiness of the chief architect, Pierre L'Enfant, work on "Federal City" (soon to be named Washington, in the President's honor) was going forward. And the Union was growing: Vermont was admitted in 1791, Kentucky in 1792, Tennessee in 1796. In 1794 General "Mad Anthony" Wayne put an end to a series of humiliating frontier reverses by routing the massed Indian tribes at Fallen Timbers in Ohio. In the same year the "Whiskey Rebellion" in Western Pennsylvania—a protest against Hamilton's hated excise tax—fizzled out when President Washington sent a militia force into the disturbed counties.

Yet troubles multiplied. Washington's show of force in Pennsylvania was interpreted by some as brutality, or as a proof that the President did what Hamilton recommended. Jefferson actually told Washington that Hamilton meant "to dismount him from being the head of the nation and to make him the head of a party."

The tone of the press began to irritate the President. Some newspapers were so unctuously flattering that they embarrassed him. Others, echoing Jefferson's position, were waspishly unfriendly. The President, they complained, was becoming either the leader or the dupe of the Federalist party. He was certainly not a dupe, and he did not mean to become leader of a faction. But little by little, despite himself, he became identified with the Federalist viewpoint.

Another difficulty was that good men were more and more reluctant to take posts in government. The work was exacting, the glamour was wearing off, and the pay was too low for persons without private incomes. Hamilton, with the need to support a family, left the Treasury in January, 1795; Jefferson, finding himself in increasing disagreement with Washington and Madison, had gone back to private life a whole year earlier. And even the talented John Marshall of Virginia, who was later to serve thirty-four years as Chief Justice of the United States Supreme Court, had to refuse a Presidential invitation to serve as Attorney General for financial reasons.

But George Washington never faltered. He and the Federalists faced a barrage of criticism when he decided to send John Jay to London to negotiate a new treaty with Britain. The step was necessary, if the British were ever to be made to evacuate the posts they were still holding in the West on American soil, and if better trading terms were to be obtained.

John Jay returned from England to discover he had been elected Governor of New York.

Jay was a known Federalist, however, and the treaty he sent back in 1795 enraged the Jeffersonians. It seemed to buy British friendship by sacrificing America's rights. Washington was himself disappointed. But he signed the treaty, as the best that could be obtained at the moment. In the uproar that went on through 1795 and 1796 over Jay's Treaty, few gave the administration credit for the diplomatic triumph of Thomas Pinckney's treaty with Spain during the same period. Under its provisions, Spain recognized American western and southern boundary claims, and guaranteed Americans free navigation of the Mississippi River with the right to deposit goods at Spanish-held New Orleans for the next three years, or longer if necessary.

The great majority of Americans continued to admire and even revere George Washington. But party strife mounted. There were some extraordinary displays of Gallomania. If the President had cared to, he could have attended, in the Philadelphia of 1794, a gruesome representation of the guillotining of Louis XVI, at the climax of which "the head falls in a basket, and the lips, which are first red, turn blue." Republicans apparently applauded, to show their sympathy with the French Revolution.

Still painful to the President were the growing attacks in newspapers and the defection of onetime admirers such as Tom Paine (who was to call him "treacherous" and a "hypocrite"). He complained bitterly in his correspondence of 1796 at being "buffited in the public prints by a set of infamous scribblers." Journalists like Benjamin Franklin Bache were speaking of him in "exaggerated and indecent terms as could scarcely be applied to a Nero; a notorious defaulter; or even to a common pickpocket."

Washington had cause to be angry. Bache was not only venomous: he was unscrupulous enough to reprint—as genuine—some letters supposedly written by General Washington during the Revolutionary War, but actually forged by the British to blacken his name. The President knew he had done his best. Perhaps he did not quite realize that a two-party system was emerging, and therefore he tended to treat the opposition as if it were wicked instead of merely critical. In practice, he recognized and even encouraged the situation by starting to appoint only Federalists to Government posts.

Certainly the discords of his second administration convinced him that he had served long enough. Eight years was almost an eternity in a position so exalted, so novel, and so lonely. By the late summer of 1796 he made his decision known. He was to retire from the Presidency and seek peace in whatever years remained to him at Mount Vernon.

He looked up the old notes for his projected farewell address of 1792 and recast them with the aid of Alexander Hamilton and John Jay. The revised document, first printed in the Philadelphia *Daily American Advertiser* on September 18, 1796, bore the marks of his recent ordeal. It contained sharp words on the "baneful effects of the Spirit of Party," and on "the insidious wiles of foreign influence." But it has also proved to be one of the timeless documents of American history, and an epitome of all that was best in his own conception of his nation's journey toward greatness.

"With me," he declared, "a predominant motive has been, to endeavor to gain time to our country to settle and mature its yet recent institutions, and to progress without interruption to that degree of strength and consistency which is necessary to give it, humanly speaking, the command of its own fortunes."

He had played for time, and successfully. He had been dignified, straightforward, cautious, and shrewd. Wiser than all his advisers, he had not sought to force the pace. He had avoided being too friendly with either of the powerful European contenders, England and France, and yet had tried not to give offense to them. He had seen the Union grow quietly but rapidly. He had stuck to a duty that he perhaps never really enjoyed in any of its aspects, until with a good conscience he could make way for someone else.

Without doubt, Martha Washington shared his relief on retirement. She probably appreciated the well-paved streets, the sophisticated shops, and stylish society of Philadelphia. But official life was a strain. It would be delightful to relax among old neighbors at Mount Vernon—although alas, many former friends were now dead or dispersed.

The newly-elected President was John Adams, the candidate of the Federalist faction. The Democratic-Republican nominee, Thomas Jefferson, had come within three electoral votes of winning and would serve as the new Vice-President. In the months between the election of November, 1796 and the inauguration of March, 1797, George Washington carried on calmly. His annual address in December recommended some favorite ideas to Congress. He wanted a national university where young Americans could learn "the science of Government," a navy, and a military academy.

On March 3, 1797, he gave a dinner for his successor. The next day he watched the inauguration of the new President, content to note in his diary little more than the temperature: "Mercury at 41." Chilly for John Adams perhaps, but not for the outgoing President. Adams, suddenly apprehensive and perhaps a little jealous of his majestic predecessor, described the occasion to his wife Abigail:

A solemn scene it was indeed, and it was made more affecting to me by the presence of the General, whose countenance was . . . serene and unclouded. . . . He seemed to me to enjoy a triumph over me. Methought I heard him say "Ay! I am fairly out and you fairly in."

Returning at last to Mount Vernon, Washington easily slips into his former routine a daily tour of his estate. Above, he converses with a farm hand during the harvest season.

8

DEATH OF A HERO, BIRTH OF A LEGEND

The Washingtons remained in Philadelphia for a few days after John Adams' inauguration to settle their personal affairs in the Capital. The son of Lafayette, a boy of seventeen, was staying in their house, and he and his tutor accompanied them when they finally left the city on March 9 for the seven-day coach journey to Mount Vernon.

The first few weeks of homecoming were not exactly tranquil. To the ex-President's keen eye, much was in need of repair. He wrote cheerfully in a letter: "I am already surrounded by Joiners, Masons, and Painters. . . . I have scarcely a room to put a friend into, or to sit in myself, without the Music of hammers, or the odoriferous smell of Paint."

As soon as the mansion's rooms were in order the visitors began to arrive, "as they say," he wrote, "out of respect to me. Pray, would not the word curiosity answer as well?" The world was still curious to see the great hero and statesman and he was too hospitable to deny a welcome.

A pleasant account of a typical visit has been left by the artist Benjamin Latrobe, who had turned up at Mount Vernon in 1796 with a letter of introduction from one of Washington's nephews. The President greeted Latrobe warmly and invited him to stay for dinner. Washington, the artist noted:

. . . has something uncommonly . . . commanding . . . in his walk, his address, his figure, and his countenance. . . He is about sixty-four but appears some years younger. . . He was sometimes silent for many minutes. . . . He appeared to enjoy a humorous observation, and made several himself. He laughed heartily some times. . . .

Mrs. Washington delighted Latrobe, and he was obviously entranced by their very pretty granddaughter, Nelly Custis, who among her many accomplishments was learning to play the harpsichord. The atmosphere was that of a well-to-do, good-natured Virginia planter's family.

Gilbert Stuart's famous portrait of George Washington was painted in 1796. This replica is one of sixty-two by the artist.

Benjamin Latrobe depicted the Washingtons at tea on the piazza of Mount Vernon.

Yet Washington was wearier than his visitors realized. He and Martha had given up dancing, of which he had once been fond. He no longer went fox-hunting, though he still rose early, breakfasted at seven, and afterward rode around his plantations on horseback. In a letter of May, 1797, he confessed to a friend that he had not much energy left by the end of the day. He meant each evening to sit down and answer letters:

. . . but when the lights are brought, I feel tired and disinclined to engage in this work, conceiving that the next night will do as well. The next comes, and with it the same causes for postponement . . . and so on . . . I have not looked into a book since I came home. . .

Gradually his health improved. He became eager to arrange the mass of public papers he had accumulated, and contentedly occupied himself with farming details. There were small domestic crises and pleasures to record in his diary. His cook ran off, a man came to tune Nelly's harpsichord, he and Martha dined in Alexandria, and the flow of visitors continued. Sally Fairfax, the girl he had admired long ago, wrote from England, where she was living as a widow.

All too soon his peace was disturbed. John Adams was finding out for himself that a President's life was full of woe. The French were acting with such extraordinary hostility that the two countries were almost at war. American and French warships were firing on one another; at sea, if not on land, there was what amounted to an undeclared war.

The more extreme Federalists were clamoring for a fight with America's former ally. Adams struggled to resist their pressure. But, while he sought a diplomatic solution to the crisis, he felt compelled to make some display of armed force. The United States must raise an army, or at least prepare to do so. Washington was the obvious choice to command it. In July, 1798, a letter from President Adams reached Mount Vernon, nominating George Washington to head America's new, provisional army.

Washington was irritated that Adams had not properly consulted him beforehand. He was afraid that critics would accuse him of refusing to relinquish the limelight. It may even have appeared a little ridiculous to him to have presented a Farewell Address and then come back on stage. But Washington could hardly refuse. The only proviso he made was that he should not be called into the field unless the threatened emergency actually arrived.

In the next few months the General was busy once more with military correspondence. He attended military parades in Virginia and even made a trip to Philadelphia for a discussion with the Secretary of War. But gradually the French became less hostile and the tension eased. Washington's thoughts turned back to Mount Vernon. His step-granddaughter Nelly Custis was married to his favorite nephew, Lawrence Lewis, on February 22, 1799. According to legend, Nelly asked the General to wear his splendid new uniform for the occasion but he preferred to dress in the old Continental blue and buff of the days of 1776.

Several times that year he spoke of the likelihood that he had not much longer to live. In July, 1799, he made his will without the aid of his secretary, Tobias Lear. It covered twenty-eight pages on both sides, written in his firm, legible handwriting; no one reading it could have thought its author was a failing man. Yet in less than six months he was dead (only two weeks after a baby was born to Nelly and Lawrence Lewis).

The end came swiftly. On December 12 he rode out for several hours to inspect his farms. It was a cold snowy day. Fond of punctuality at meals, he sat down to dine without changing his wet clothes. The next day he had a chill and a sore throat. His condition quickly worsened, until he could only breathe with a painful effort. The household tried out the primitive remedies of the time—including a nauseating potion of vinegar, molasses, and butter—but he could not swallow.

His old companion of the 1784 journey to the Western bounty lands, Dr. Craik, was called in, and then two more doctors from the neighborhood.

A 1798 recruiting poster calls for troops to defend America against "hostile designs of foreign enemies"—in this case, France.

141

An early nineteenth-century print (above) shows Washington dying attended by Martha and his physicians. Originally buried in the old family vault (left), his body was removed in 1831 to a brick tomb at Mount Vernon. Opposite, a December, 1799, procession in Philadelphia commemorates Washington's death.

The only treatment they could agree upon, bloodletting, weakened him further. Medical treatment of the period was powerless to deal with an infection that could almost certainly have been cured by modern methods.

He was under no illusion. "Doctor," he is supposed to have said to Dr. Craik, "I die hard but I am not afraid to go." While he was still able to speak, in a hoarse whisper, he issued final instructions about his will. As night came on December 14, 1799, the three doctors, Martha, Tobias Lear, and his Negro house servant Christopher watched at the bedside in helpless anguish. Almost the last gesture Washington made was to feel the pulse in his wrist. The little group gathered around him, and saw his lips move as he tried to count his pulse rate. Two hours before midnight he

was dead. He was just two months short of being sixty-eight. On December 18 George Washington was buried in the simple family vault on the slope of Mount Vernon.

Posterity did not bring about everything he had hoped. The national university which he wished to see established in the District of Columbia, and for which he left a bequest, was never built. But the military academy he had recommended was founded at West Point in 1802. The political scene of his final years had been confused and full of animosity. For a decade or so following his death, the Federalists tried to claim him as their own particular patron saint; as a result, some of the Jeffersonian Republicans were apt to question his greatness. Once his formidable presence was removed, certain

A NEW NATION'S
NEW CAPITAL

Pierre Charles L'Enfant was commissioned by President Washington to draw up plans for the new Federal City. L'Enfant's 1792 scheme (below right) had two focal points: the Capitol and the President's mansion. Broad avenues cut through the grid plan to provide long vistas of important buildings. The architectural competition for the Capitol was won by William Thornton, whose design (below) was dominated by a shallow dome with a classical portico and two symmetrical wings. At right, the section of the Capitol completed by 1800, corresponding to the right wing of Thornton's east elevation, is inspected by visitors.

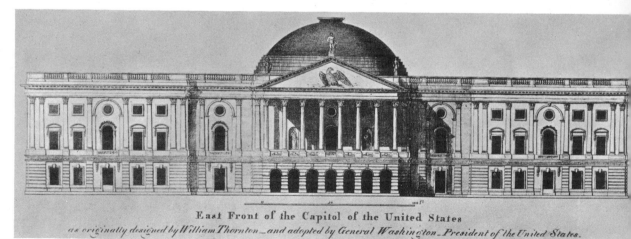

East Front of the Capitol of the United States
as originally designed by William Thornton — and adopted by General Washington — President of the United States.

associates confided in one another that they had long thought his reputation exaggerated.

But the nation as a whole mourned his death. Foreigners commented with awe that George Washington was a hero of almost sacred fame. By degrees all political groups and all regions acknowledged him as "Pater Patriae"—Father of his Country.

In time George Washington came to mean all things to all people.

In the growing crisis over slavery, the North could praise him because he had freed his own slaves in his will, and because he emphasized *Union*. To the South he was a magnificent representative of the Old Dominion, Virginia. Mounted on horseback, he was the pictorial symbol at the center of the Confederate Seal.

Almost every religious denomination could lay claim to him too—the Episcopalians because he had worshiped in their church, the Presbyterians or Baptists because of rumors that he had secretly joined them. Others, including freethinkers, admired him for his marked tolerance.

In the national memory, then, George Washington came to represent the Revolution, the Constitution, and the United States itself. He was the maker and the model, the example and the symbol. It was only fitting that so many places—streets, squares, towns, counties, states, and mountains—should be named after him.

Nor is it surprising that so many people have written about him, or

145

that they have concocted so many stories to try to express their sense of his sterling quality. Unfortunately, the effect of many of these stories, so firmly embedded in American folklore, has been to make him unreal. Historians have protested that few of the stories have any basis in fact.

The tale of little George and the cherry tree was probably an invention of the early biographer Mason Weems. There is no foundation either in such well-known folk beliefs as the one that has George Washington designing the American flag in company with Betsy Ross. The famous painting by Emanuel Leutze—of Washington crossing the Delaware in a small boat surrounded by chunks of ice—is a romantic and picturesque version of a scene that probably looked a good deal different. Even the fairly accurate portrait done by Gilbert Stuart in Washington's later years is misleading because it fastened in most minds a notion of a stern and weary man who somehow looks as if he had been born old.

George Washington had virtues that were solid rather than spectacular. He was sensible rather than dazzling. No one would pretend that he was capable of as much eloquence or had as quick a sense of humor as his illustrious successor Abraham Lincoln, who shares with him the same lofty place in the pantheon of American heroes.

Thomas Jefferson gave the perfect summary of George Washington's personality in a tribute written in a letter of 1814:

He was incapable of fear, meeting personal dangers with the calmest unconcern. Perhaps the strongest feature in his character was prudence, never acting until every . . . consideration, was maturely weighed; refraining if he saw a doubt, but, when once decided, going through with his purpose, whatever obstacles opposed. His integrity was most pure, his justice the most inflexible I have ever known . . . Washington's was the singular destiny and merit, of leading the armies of his country successfully through an arduous war, for the establishment of its independence; of conducting its councils through the birth of a government, new in its forms and principles, until it had settled down into a quiet and orderly train; and of scrupulously obeying the laws through the whole of his career . . .

As Jefferson concluded, the history of the world furnishes no other such example; and people of all lands came to admire him for what he had done and for what he had been.

Washington held out to every nation the hope against hope—that it was possible for men of true nobility to emerge, to rule wisely, and to remain uncorrupt. This is an achievement still to be marveled at, and never to be taken for granted. His life and the meaning of his life became as vast as the United States itself. In time he became merged with the nation he had helped create.

A weeping soldier and disconsolate Liberty mourn for Washington in the sentimental engraving of 1800, opposite. Angels and cupids carry symbols of his earthly deeds; his portrait is held by a helmeted goddess.

TRENTON
PRINCETOWN
MONMOUTH
YORKTOWN.

PATER
PATRIÆ.

Sacred to the Memory of the
truly Illustrious
GEORGE WASHINGTON, Renowned in
War, Great in the Senate, and
possessed of every Qualification
to render him worthy the Title of
a GREAT and GOOD MAN.

BORN Feb. 22. 1732. Ob. Dec. 14. 1799.

LIBRARY OF CONGRESS

A mess kit with assorted utensils accompanied Washington to his wartime headquarters.

AMERICAN HERITAGE PUBLISHING CO., INC.

James Parton, *President*

Joseph J. Thorndike, *Editor in Chief*

Richard M. Ketchum, *Editorial Director, Book Division*

Stephen W. Sears, *Editor, Education Department*

Irwin Glusker, *Art Director*

AMERICAN HERITAGE JUNIOR LIBRARY

JOSEPH L. GARDNER, *Managing Editor*

Janet Czarnetzki, *Art Director*

Annette Welles, *Copy Editor*

Mary Leverty, *Picture Researcher*

Nancy Simon, *Editorial Researcher*

ACKNOWLEDGMENTS

The Editors are indebted to the following individuals and institutions for their generous assistance in preparing this book:

Bangor Public Library, Bangor, Maine—Robert C. Woodward
Colonial Williamsburg—Marguerite Gignilliat
Library of Congress—Virginia Daiker, Dorothy Eaton, Walter W. Ristow
Mount Vernon Ladies' Association of the Union—Christine Meadows
Museum of the City of New York—Mrs. Henriette Beal
New-York Historical Society—Rachel Minick, Carolyn Scoon
Washington and Lee University, Lexington, Virginia —John Hughes

FURTHER READING

Bakeless, John, *Turncoats, Traitors and Heroes.* Lippincott, 1959.

Boorstin, Daniel J., *The Americans; the Colonial Experience.* Random House, 1958.

Bridenbaugh, Carl, *Cities in Revolt, 1743–1776.* Knopf, 1955.
——— *Seat of Empire.* Holt, 1958.

Cleland, Hugh, *George Washington in the Ohio Valley.* Pittsburgh, 1956.

Cunliffe, Marcus, *George Washington, Man and Monument.* Little, Brown, 1958.

Flexner, Thomas, *George Washington, the Forge of Experience, 1732–1775.* Little, Brown, 1965.

Freeman, Douglas Southall, *George Washington.* Vols. I–VI, J. A. Carroll and M. W. Ashworth, Vol. VII, Scribner's, 1948–1957.

Ketchum, Richard M., ed., *The American Heritage Book of the Revolution.* American Heritage, 1958.

Knollenberg, Bernhard, *George Washington; the Virginia Period 1732–1775.* Duke, 1964.

Lancaster, Bruce, *From Lexington to Liberty.* Doubleday, 1955.

McDonald, Forrest, *E. Pluribus Unum: the Foundation of the American Republic 1766–1790.* Houghton Mifflin, 1965.

Miller, John C., *The Federalist Era.* Harper, 1960.

Morris, Richard B., *The Peacemakers: the Great Powers and American Independence.* Harper, 1965.

Nettels, Curtis P., *George Washington and American Independence.* Little, Brown, 1951.

Osgood, Herbert L., *The American Colonies in the Eighteenth Century.* Columbia, 1924.

Plumb, J. H., *The First Four Georges.* Macmillan, 1957.

Rossiter, Clinton, *Seedtime of the Republic.* Harcourt, 1953.

Schacher, Nathan, *The Founding Fathers.* Capricorn, 1954.

Thane, Elswyth, *Mount Vernon is Ours.* Duell, Sloan & Pearce, 1966.

Van Doren, Carl, *The Great Rehearsal.* Viking, 1961.

Ward, Christopher, *The War of Revolution.* 2 Vols., Macmillan, 1952.

Washington, George, *The Washington Papers,* Saul K. Padover, ed., Harper, 1955.

Weems, Mason L., *The Life of George Washington,* Marcus Cunliffe, ed., Harper, 1962.

Wertenbaker, Thomas, *The Golden Age of Colonial Structure.* New York University, 1949.

White, Leonard D., *The Federalists.* Macmillan, 1948.

Wright, Louis B., *The Atlantic Frontier.* Knopf, 1951.

These 1796 companion portraits of the Washingtons by James Sharples today hang at Mount Vernon.

INDEX

Bold face indicates pages on which illustrations appear

A

Adams, Abigail, 126, 137
Adams, John, 14, 54, 56, 57, **57,** 59, 70, **71,** 105, 114, 120, 125, **125,** 131, 136, 137, 138, 140, 141
    quoted, 137
Adams, Samuel, 45, 57, **57**
Albany, N.Y., 79
Alexandria, Va., 19, 140
Allegheny Mountains, 20, 23
Allegheny River, 23
Allen, Ethan, 63
André, Maj. John, 94, **94,** 95
Annapolis, Md., 16, 104, 105
Anti-Federalists, 130, 131, 136
Arnold, Benedict, 63, 66, 95
Articles of Confederation, 94, 114, 116

B

Bache, Benjamin Franklin, 135
Baltimore, Md., 76
Barbados, B.W.I., 19
Belhaven, Va., *see* Alexandria
Belvoir, 16, 37
Bennington, Vt., 87
Bill of Rights, 119, 126
Billy Lee, 6, **7**
Blue Ridge Mountains, 17
Boston, Mass., 56, 59, 64, 68, 102
    British in, **48–49,** 49, 54, 55, 63, 65
    Continental Army in, 61–62, 66
Boston Tea Party, 46, **46,** 47–48
Braddock, Gen. Edward, 20, **20–21,** 27, **27,** 28, 30, **30–31,** 111
Brandywine Creek, 82, 83

British, fleet, 64, **68–69,** 69, 91, **92–93,** 93, 97
    French war with, 23, 26, 27, 29, 32, 41, 131
    military camp, **74–75**
    military forces, 61–102, *passim*
Brooklyn, N.Y., 70
Brooklyn Heights, N.Y., 70
Bunker Hill, Battle of, 63, **63**
Burgoyne, Gen. John, 79, 82, 86, 87

C

Cadwalder, Gen. John, 89
Cambridge, Mass., 59, 63, 68
Camden, S.C., 97
Canada, 20, 24, 26, 63, 79, 86, 87
    American invasion of, 63, 65, 66
Cape Henry, Va., 93

Cavalier, Robert, Sieur de La Salle, 22
Champlain, Lake, 63
  Hudson River route, 79
Chapman, John Gadsby, 19
  painting by, **18**
Chappel, Alonzo
  painting by, **104**
Charles I of England, 45
Charles River, 63
Charleston, S.C., 69, 79, 94, 96, 102, 134
Charlestown Neck, Mass., 63, 66
Charlotte, Queen, 42, **42**
Chastellux, Chevalier, 103
Cherry tree legend, 7, 15, **15**, 146
Chesapeake Bay, 82, 100
Chew House, 83, **83**
Cincinnati, Society of the, 115, 116
Cincinnatus, 109
Clinton, Sir Henry, 79, 87, 89, 91, 94, 96, 97, 100, 103
College of William and Mary, 14
Colonies, 29, 54, 56
  British taxation of, 41, 44, 45, 47
  England and, 59, 62, 69
  trade with, 44, 50, 55
Columbia University, 36
Common Sense, quote from, 69
Concord, Mass., Battle of, 56
Connecticut, 61, 111
Constitution of the United States, 114, **116**, 118, 126
  drafting, 116–117
  provisions, 117–118
  signing, 118
  ratification, 119, 123
    cartoon of, **119**
Constitutional Convention, 116–117, 118, **118**
  Committee on Style, 117
Continental Army, 56, 59, 61 105 *passim*, 116
  conditions in, 65–66, 94–95
  riflemen, 65
  uniforms, 67, **67**
Continental Congress, First, 50, 51–54, 56
Continental Congress, Second, 55, **55**, 56, 59, 61, 62, 63, 66, 123
Convention of Saratoga, 87
Conway, Thomas, 89
Copley, John Singleton
  painting by, **57**
Cornwallis, Gen. Lord, 76, 77, 93, 96, 97
  defeat at Yorktown, 98, **98–99**, 100, 102
Cowpens, S.C., 97
Craigie House, 64
Craik, Dr., 111, 141, 143
Cunliffe, Marcus, 7

Custis, Daniel Parke, 33
Custis, George Washington Parke
  painting by, **78**
Custis, Jack, 33, 36, 47, 100, 107
Custis, Nelly Calvert, 36, 138, 140, 141
Custis, Patsy, 33

D

Declaration of Independence, 69, 70, 88
  drafting committee, 70, **70**
Delaware River, Washington crossing, 7, 60, **60–61**, 73, 76, **77**, 146
Democratic Republicans, *see* Anti-Federalists
Dinwiddie, Gov. Robert, 23, 25, **25**, 32, 38
District of Columbia, 143
Dorchester Heights, Mass., 66, 68
Dunmore, Lord, 47, 49, 55, 56

E

East India Co., 47
East River, 70, 73
England, *see* Great Britain
English Civil War, 45
Epsewasson, 12, 16
Erie, Lake, 23, 25
Estaing, Comte d', 91

F

Fairfax, Anne, 16
Fairfax, Bryan, 50, 51
  quoted, 50
Fairfax, George William, 49, 50
Fairfax, Lord, 16–17
Fairfax, Sally, 16, 140
Fairfax, Col. William, 16
Fairfax County, Va., 38, 55
Fairfaxes, 19, 20, 37
Fallen Timbers, Ohio, 134
Fauntleroy, Betsy, 16
Federal City, 6, 126, 134, 144
Federal Hall, 122, **122**
Federalists, 130, 131, 134, 136, 140, 143
  cartoon of, **130**
Ferry Farm, 13, 38
Forbes, Gen. John, 32
Fort Clinton, 95
Fort Cumberland, 27, **132–133**, 133
Fort Duquesne, 26, 27, 28, 32, 33
Fort Le Boeuf, 23, 25
Fort Lee, 73
Fort Necessity, 26, 27, 59, 111
Fort Pitt, 32, **32**
Fort Robertdeau, 110, **110**
Fort Ticonderoga, 63, 68, 79, 86
Fort Washington, 73
France, 20, 62, 132, 141

New World empire of, 20, 32
  Reign of Terror in, 129
  royal family of, 128, **128**, 129
Franklin, Benjamin, 57, **57**, 70, **71**, 87, 88, 105, 117
  quoted, 114
Franklin, state of, 111
Fraunces, Sam, 122
Fraunces' Tavern, 105
Frederick County, Va., 38
Fredericksburg, Va., 13
French, American allies of, 87–88, 91, 93, 94
  American undeclared war with, 140–141
  British war with, 23, 26, 27, 29, 41, 88, 131
  Canadian provinces, 41
  fleet, **92–93**, 93
  Indians and, 20–22, 26, 27, 41
  Revolution, 129, 131, 135
  troops, 93, **93**
  Yorktown siege, **98–99**
French and Indian War, 23–32 *passim*, 41, 62
Frost, J. O. J.
  painting by, **60–61**

G

Gage, Gen. Thomas, 47, 49, 56, 59, 63, 65, 86, 103
Gates, Gen. Horatio, 62, 87, 89, **89**, 97
Genêt, Edmond Charles, 132, 134
George II of England, 22
George III of England, 41, 42, **42**, **43**, 45, 56, 59, 69, 79
Georgetown, D.C., 126
Georgia, 54, 82, 94, 96
German troops, *see* Hessians
Germantown, Pa., Battle of, 82, 83, **83**
Gist, Christopher, 25, 26, **26**
Gladstone, William E., 7
Grasse, Adm. de, 100
Great Britain, 11, 20, 26, 47, 48, 51, 56, 59, 62, 69, 102, 132
  colonial sympathizers in, 44, 46
  political cartoon, 40, **40–41**
Great Dismal Swamp, 36, **37**, 38
Great Lakes, 20
Green Mountain Boys, 63, 87
Greene, Gen. Nathanael, 61, 62, 78, **78**, 82, **96**, 97, 102, 107
Guilford Court House, N.C., 97
Gulf of Mexico, 20

H

Halifax, Nova Scotia, 68, 69
Hamilton, Alexander, 89, 95, 100, 116, 117, 123, **123**, **124–125**, 125, 129, 130, **130**, 131, 134, 136

Hampton, Va., 16
Harlem Heights, N.Y., Battle of, 72, **72,** 73
Harvard College, 64, 126
Head of Elk, Md., 82
Henry, Patrick, 38, 44, 45, 50, 51, **51,** 56, 116
Hessians, 60, 70, 72, 76, 83
regiments, **74–75,** 75
Honeywood, St. John
water color by, **58**
Houdon, Jean, 110
Howe, Adm. Lord, 70
cartoon of, **86**
Howe, Sir William, 65, 68, 69, **69,** 70, 72, 73, 76, 79, 82, 83, 86, 89, 103
cartoon of, **86**
Hudson River, 73, 87, 95
Humphreys, David, 122

I

Intolerable Acts, 48, 54

J

Jackson, Andrew, 97
Jackson, Maj. William, 122
James River, 15, 97, 114
Jay, John, 105, 115, 123, **124–125,** 125, 134, 135, **135,** 136
Jay, Mrs. John, **124–125,** 125
Jay's Treaty, 135
Jefferson, Thomas, 14, 57, **57,** 69, 70, **71,** 97, 123, **123, 124–125,** 125, 127, 129, 130, 131, 132, 134, 136, 146
cartoon of, **130**
quoted, 146
Jeffersonian Republicans, 135, 143

K

Kalb, Baron de, 97
Kentucky, 134
King's College, 36, 47
Kingston, N.Y., 87
Kip's Bay, 72
Knox, Henry, 68, 119, 123, **123**

L

Lafayette, Marquis de, 89, **92,** 93, 97, 102, **102,** 108, 109, **109,** 119
son of, 138
Latrobe, Benjamin, 138
drawing by, **37**
quoted, 138
water color by, **140**
Laurens, Henry, 105
Lear, Tobias, 111, 141, 143
Lee, Gen. Charles, 61, 62, 76, **76,** 89, 91
Lee, Henry "Light-Horse Harry," quoted, 7

L'Enfant, Pierre Charles, 134, 144
Leutze, Emanuel, 7, 8, 146
paintings by, **4–5, 77**
Lewis, Lawrence, 141
Lexington, Mass., Battle of, 56, 58, **58**
Lincoln, Abraham, 146
Little Hunting Creek, 12, 13
Livingston, Robert, 70, **71**
Long Island, N.Y., 68, **68–69,** 70, 73, 82
Louis XVI of France, 135
Louisiana, 20, 24

M

Maclay, Sen. William, 126, 128
quoted, 127
Madison, James, 114, 116, 117, 123, 128, 134
Maine, 82
Manhattan, N.Y., 70, 72, 73, 79, 120
Maps,
Battle of Princeton, **80–81**
Battle of Trenton, **80–81**
Boston Harbor, **66**
British Colonies, **23–24**
Federal City, **145**
New York campaign, **73**
Philadelphia Campaign, **82**
West Point fortifications, **95**
Yorktown, **101**
See also, George Washington
Marshall, John, 134
Maryland, 65, 82, 100, 114
Mason, George, 46, 47, 50, 117
Massachusetts, 47, 49, 54, 61, 62
soldiers, 56
Mississippi River, 135
Mississippi River Valley, 20, 38
Mohawk River Valley, 79, 87
Monmouth Court House, N.J., 89, 94
Battle of, **4–5,** 8, **90**
Monogahela, Battle of the, 20, **20–21,** 27–29, 30, **30–31**
Monongahela River, 22
Montgomery, Gen. Richard, 63, 64, **64,** 66
Montreal, Canada, 63
Morgan, Daniel, 65, 95, **96,** 97
Morristown, N.J., 77, 79, 94
Mount Vernon, 7, 12, 16, 19, 27, 33, 34, **35,** 36, 38, 41, 50, 51, 55, 59, 88, 91, 100, 105, **106,** 107, 108, 109, **109,** 110, 111, **112–113,** 113, 114, 116, 119, 120, 126, 138, 140, **140,** 141
Mount Vernon Ladies Assoc., 113

N

New England, 61, 79, 126

New Hampshire, 61, 119
New Haven, Conn., 59
New Jersey, 73, 74, 77, 79, 82, 100
New Orleans, La., 135
Battle of, 97
New York, N.Y., 59, 61, 62, 68, 69, 73, 76, 79, 87, 89, 91, 96, 97, 100, 120, 126
British invasion of, 56, 70
harbor, **front endsheet,** 8
Newburgh, N.Y., 103
Newport, R.I., 91
Norfolk, Va., 16
North, Lord, 42, 103
caricature of, **42**
North Carolina, 111, 123
Northern Neck, Va., 117

O

Ohio Co., 22
Ohio River, 111
forks of, 22, 23, 26, 27, 28
Ohio Valley, 22, 32, 41
bounty lands, 38
Osgood, Samuel, 123
Oswego, N.Y., 79
Otis, James, 45

P

Paine, Thomas, 69, 135
Paoli, Pa., 83
Peale, Charles Willson
portraits by, **38, 39, 57, 89, 96**
Peekskill, N.Y., 73, 82
Pell's Point, N.Y., 73
Pennsylvania, 23, 65, 87, 134
Philadelphia, Pa., 50, 51, **52–53,** 53, 54, 56, 59, 61, 76, 79, 82, 83, 86, 89, 103, 115, 127, **127,** 135, 138, 141, 142, **143**
Pinckney, Thomas, 135
Pitt, William, 32
Pittsburgh, Pa., 32
Potomac River, 12, 15, 17, 19, 37, 51, 111, 126
Great Falls of, 111, 115, **115**
Potomac River Co., 114
Princeton, N.J., 77, 79, 80, **80–81,** 97
Putnam, Gen. Israel, 61, 62, 70

Q

Quartering Act, 45, **45**
Quebec, Canada, 63, 64, 95

R

Raleigh Tavern, 49
Randolph, Edmund, 123
Randolph, John, 51
Randolph, Peyton, 50, 51, **51,** 56
Rappahannock River, 13, 15, 17
Revolutionary War, 61–105 *pas-*

sim, 111, 114, 135
Rhode Island, 61, 123, 126
Rochambeau, Comte de, 93, **93**, 97, 100
Ross, Betsy, 146
Rossiter, Thomas
  painting by, **118**
Royal Navy, 15

S

St. Lawrence River, 20, 63
St Leger, Gen Barry, 79, 87
Saratoga, N.Y., 87, 95, 97, 100
  British surrender at, 87, **87**, 88
Savannah, Ga., 102
Schuyler, Gen. Philip, 61, 62, 79, 82, 87, 95
Shays, Capt. Daniel, 116
  rebellion of, 116
Shenandoah Valley, 17, 19, 62
Sherman, Roger, 70, **71**
Spain, 91
  treaty with United States, 135
Stamp Act, 42, 44, 45, 46
  Bostonians defy, **44**
Stark, John, 87
Staten Island, N.Y., **68–69**, 69, 70
Steuben, Baron von, 85, 97
Stuart, Gilbert, 7, 107, 138, 146
  portrait by, **139**
Sullivan, Gen. John, 61, 70, 83, 91, 95

T

Tarleton, Banastre, 97
Tennessee, 134
Thornton, William, 144
Throgs Neck, N.Y., 73
Townshend Acts, 45, 46, 47
Treaty of Alliance of 1778, 88, 93, 132
Trenton, N.J., 60, 76, 78, 79, 97, 117, 120, **120–21**
  Battle of, **cover**, 8, **78, 80–81**
  Hessian surrender at, 8, **back endsheet**
Trinity Church, 122, **122**
Trumbull, John
  paintings by, **cover, 70, 130, back endsheet**
Truro Parish, Va., 38

U

United States, 70, 88, 111, 126, 132, 134, 140
  Capitol, 144, **144**
  Congress, 76, 79, 82, 87, 88–89, 94, 111
  disunity in, 128–136
  independence, 105
  Government, 114, 126, 129
  recruiting poster, **141**

Senate Journal, 131, **131**

V

Valley Forge, Pa., 82, 83, 84, **84–85**, 85, 86, 88, 89, 117
Vermont, 63, 134
Vernon, Adm. Edward, 16
Virginia, 23, 25, 26, 27, 50, 54, 61, 65, 97, 111, 114, 141
  colonial life in, 15–16, 36
  convention in Richmond, 55–56
  Council, 16, 23
  Custis's in, 33
  frontier defenses, 29
  General Assembly, 11, 15, 26, 44, 49
  Indian claims in, 17
  plantation in, 10, **10–11**
  royal colony, 11
  settlers in, 20
  Washingtons in, 11, 12

W

Wakefield, Va., 12, 13
Wall Street, 120, 122, **122**
Ward, Gen. Artemas, 61
Washington, Augustine, 11, 12, 13
Washington, Augustine, Jr., 13
Washington, Bushrod, 111
Washington, Charles, 12
Washington, Elizabeth, 12
Washington, George, **cover, endsheets, 4–5, 6, 9, 18, 20–21, 26, 34–35, 39, 60–61, 62, 77, 78, 84–85, 88, 90, 102, 104, 106, 109, 118, 120–121, 123, 124–125, 132–133, 137, 139, 140, 142, 143, 150**
  cartoon of, **130**
  Birth, 12
  Boyhood, 13, 16
  Education, 13–15
  Surveyor, 17–19
  Early military career, 23–32
  Marriage, 33, 34
  Farmer at Mount Vernon, 36–37
  In Tidewater society, 37–38
  Member, Virginia legislature, 38, 44
  British taxation and, 44, 46, 48, 49–50, 51
  Delegate, First Continental Congress, 51–54
  Delegate, Second Continental Congress, 56
  Constitutional Convention, 115, 116–118
  Commander in Chief, 56, 59
  Boston campaign, 62, 63, 64, 66, 68
  Continental Army and, 64–66, 94, 103–105

New York campaign, 69–73
New Jersey campaign, 76–79
Philadelphia campaign, 82–83
Valley Forge retreat, 83
At Monmouth Court House, 89–91
Yorktown campaign, 100–102
Farewell orders, 105
Retirement to Mount Vernon, 105, 107–111, 136, 137, 138–140
Western expansion and, 111–114
President, 119, 120 136
Inaugural address, 122–123
Cabinet of, 123, 129
Social style, 124–126
Political parties and, 129–135
Newspaper attacks on, 134, 135
Farewell address, 128, 136, 141
Provisional army head, 140–141
Death, 141–143
As a symbol, 109, 114, 119, 145–146
Biographers, 14–15, 146
Copybook, **17**
Maps by, **17, 19, 23, 27**
Quoted, 17, 26, 37, 47, 49, 51, 54, 59, 62, 65, 66, 69, 73, 88, 95, 96, 103, 109–110, 110, 114, 119, 135, 138, 140
Washington, Jane, 13
Washington, John, 11, 12
Washington, John Augustine, 12, 107
Washington, Lawrence, 12, **12,** 13, 15, 16, 17, 19, 32
Washington, Lund, 37, 88
Washington, Martha, 6, **6–7,** 33, 34, **34,** 37, 38, 59, 62, 79, 94, 109, **109,** 116, 120, **124–125,** 125, 126, 136, 138, 140, 142, **142,** 143, **150**
  quoted, 94
Washington, Mary Ball, 12, 13, 15, 38
Washington, Mildred, 12
Washington, Samuel, 12
Wayne, Gen. "Mad Anthony," 83, 134
Weems, Mason, 14, 146
West Point, N.Y., 95, 116, 143
Whiskey Rebellion, 133, 134
White Plains, N.Y., 73, 91
Williamsburg, Va., 14, 16, 23, 38, 49, 50, 100
Wilmington, Del., 82, 97, 119
Wollaston, John
  paintings by, **34, 35**

Y

York River, 15, 97
Yorktown, Va., 16, 93, 97, 98–99, **98–99,** 100
  Battle of, 102, **102**